D1486027

POL[illegible]

Between the Hamme[illegible]vil

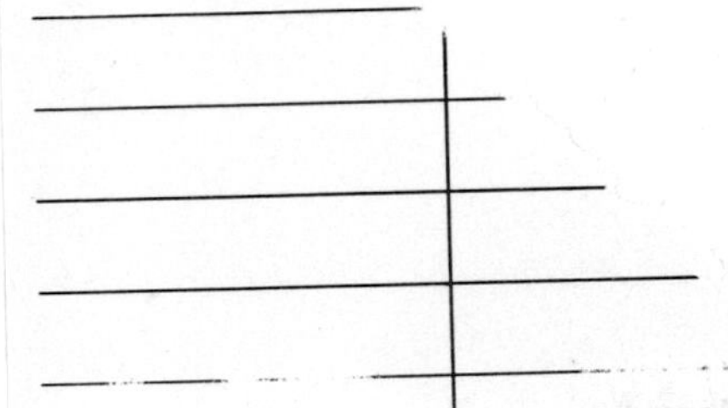

BY THE SAME AUTHOR

Spring in October, *the Polish Revolution of 1959*

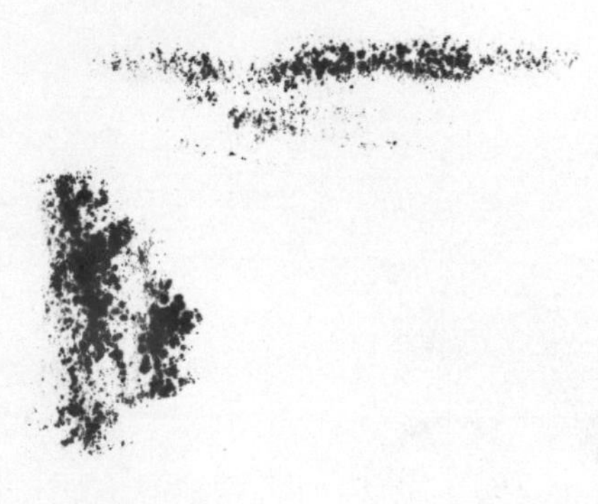

KONRAD SYROP

POLAND

Between the Hammer and the Anvil

ILLUSTRATED
AND WITH MAPS

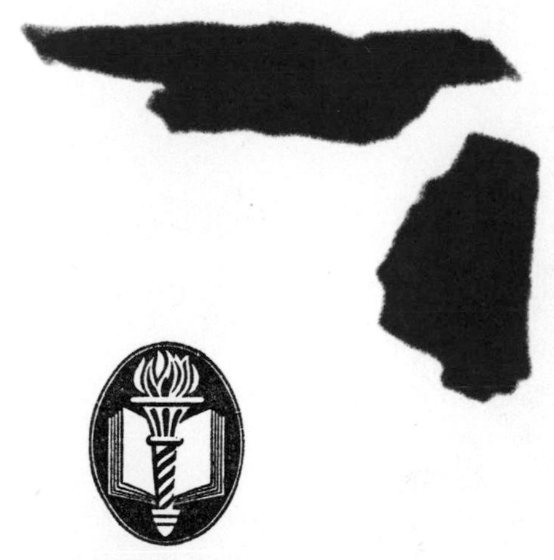

ROBERT HALE · LONDON

First published in Great Britain 1968

SBN 7091 0230 5

Robert Hale Limited
63 Old Brompton Road
London S.W.7

To my Wife

PRINTED IN GREAT BRITAIN
BY EBENEZER BAYLIS AND SON, LTD.
THE TRINITY PRESS, WORCESTER, AND LONDON

CONTENTS

PART FOUR
RISE AND FALL AGAIN

PART FIVE
HALF-FREEDOM, HALF-INDEPENDENCE

ILLUSTRATIONS

ACKNOWLEDGEMENTS

Kolowca Stanislaw (1, 3, 4); Paul Popper Limited (2, 12, 13, 14, 15, 17, 18); Henryk Romanowski (5); Radio Times Hulton Picture Library (6, 8); Keytone Press Agency (7, 9, 10, 16); Leonard Sempolinski (11); Marian Gadzalski (19).

MAPS

PREFACE

Almost everything about Poland is controversial and objectivity can only be achieved at the price of dullness. All I have attempted in this book is an honest presentation of facts and their assessment as I see them. I may add that, while making no claim to objectivity, I also have no axe to grind.

Since in the case of Poland the present is hopelessly intertwined with the past, this book does span a thousand years of history, but it is firmly focused on the present. I have tried to make it as up-to-date as possible at the time of writing.

London K.S.

AUTHOR'S NOTE

The spelling of Polish names is phonetic as far as possible. This may offend some purists but should make it easier for the non-specialist reader. The Index at the end of the book gives both the phonetic and the correct spellings as well as the German and Russian versions of place names when appropriate.

PART ONE

THE RISE OF A COMMONWEALTH

1

MILLENNIUM

Seven years of celebrations is a long period for any anniversary however important. Yet this is precisely what the Polish Government ordered in 1959 to commemorate the millennium of the foundation of the State. Even for a nation as proud of its past as the Poles, this might appear somewhat excessive. But the communist Government had at least two good reasons for organizing such prolonged festivities. There was first the legitimate uncertainty about the precise moment when Poland emerged as a state and, more important still, from the political point of view it was essential not to have the anniversary associated too closely with the millennium of Poland's adoption of Christianity which fell in 1966.

In Poland's peculiar circumstances what should have been a proud national occasion marked by innocuous historical pageants, festivals, exhibitions and perhaps some beating of the patriotic drum, turned in the end into a bitter conflict between the Church and the State and nearly led to a final showdown between the two dominant forces in the country. The reasons for this course of events are buried in Poland's long and highly controversial past.

Oddly enough the *casus belli* between the Church and the State was a letter of reconciliation. Towards the end of the Vatican Council thirty-six Polish Roman Catholic archbishops and bishops headed by the Primate, Cardinal Wyszynski, sent a letter of reconciliation to the Roman Catholic hierarchy in East and West Germany. They recalled the past unhappy Polish-German relations, recounted German crimes against Poland and also the expulsion of the Germans from Poland's present western provinces, ending with an offer of and request for forgiveness. The letter included the following sentence:

'. . . we beg to communicate to you, Reverend Brethren, as our nearest western neighbours, the joyful tidings that next year—in the year of Our Lord 1966—the Church of Christ in Poland and with her the whole Polish people will celebrate the millennium of their baptism and thereby also the thousandth anniversary of our national and State existence.'

The bishops' letter aroused the wrath of the Polish Government, who accused the episcopate of presumption, lack of patriotism, disloyalty to the State and other crimes. Retaliation followed. The proposed visit of the Pope to the millennium celebrations was cancelled, foreign bishops and even ordinary pilgrims were not allowed into the country, the Primate's passport was withdrawn so that he could not visit America as planned. When the religious celebrations came, the Government engaged in a campaign of petty restrictions. Short of banning the services and processions and arresting the bishops, the communists did everything in their power to prevent people from attending the celebrations and divert them to rival, purely secular attractions.

Meanwhile official Polish historians were at pains to contradict the bishops' statement that the introduction of Christianity marked the emergence of the Polish State. To quote one of them: 'When Mieszko I adopted Christianity the land forming his kingdom had a long history behind it and the people living in it were a nation not without a past or a culture . . . the state was not a wholly new or alien structure which arose only after the adoption of Christianity and as its consequence . . . Christianity became prevalent on the strength of the ruler's decision because its structure made it one of the levers of the machinery of Power.'[1]

One does not have to read between the lines to see how history is being used as a weapon in the present struggle between Church and State. But in fact early Polish history contained the seeds of most of her present-day problems.

It all started in the small town of Gniezno in central Poland. Today Gniezno is an unimportant provincial town of some fifty thousand inhabitants which is found only on the more detailed maps of Europe, about half way between Moscow and Paris. But more than a thousand years ago it was a castle of some consequence. Recent archaeological excavations to bring to light

[1] K. Grzybowski, 'Ten Centuries of Statehood'. Supplement to Polish *Facts and Figures*, Polish Embassy, London, 1966.

more evidence about the origins of the Polish state have revealed huge wooden and earthen ramparts dating back to the eighth century.

What happened in Poland before the year 963 is a matter of historical conjecture helped by archaeological detection, but in that year a chronicler noted that the Polish ruler, Mieszko I, was twice attacked and defeated by the Saxon Count Wichman. About that time German expansion to the east brought them to Mieszko's frontier. The stage was set for a thousand years of struggle between the two nations.

We do not know how it came about that of all the north-western Slav chieftains the Piasts, who from Gniezno ruled the tribe of the Polanie (the men of the plains), should have established their authority over neighbouring tribes and created the nucleus of the future Polish state. It is at least probable that the eastward pressure of the German barons, who saw a good chance to combine a crusading mission against the pagan Slavs with the acquisition of desirable land, had a great deal to do with it. In the case of Mieszko it may have provided the decisive stimulus. He consolidated and extended his vast domain whose frontiers coincided to a large extent with those of present-day Poland, and tried to resist the German pressure, but he was at first not powerful enough to do it alone. After his defeat by Wichman he turned for help to Otto I who had just been crowned Emperor of the Holy Roman Empire. Mieszko became 'the Emperor's friend' and undertook to pay him tribute in respect of some of his territories. This conferred a legal status on Mieszko's duchy and should have afforded him a certain measure of protection from the aggressive German barons.

Two years later Mieszko married a Christian princess from Bohemia and in 966 he himself embraced Christianity, bringing Poland into the orbit of the Church of Rome and removing the main pretext for German encroachments. However, during the next two decades he had to fight the Germans on at least three more occasions and was victorious each time; but an invasion from the east by Vladimir the Great cost Poland a border province which was to change hands several times in the future. Mieszko also entered into a temporary alliance with the Czechs, but later fought them successfully over the possession of Silesia and southern Poland.

Thus, in the first thirty years of recorded Polish history we can already see the pattern of the future: pressure from the east and the west, bad relations with the southern neighbour and the introduction of Roman Catholicism into Poland. It remained for Mieszko's eldest son and successor to complete the picture by giving birth to the dream of greatness through eastward expansion.

Poland's fate has been largely determined by her position sandwiched between two powerful states. Mieszko's deliberate decision to embrace Christianity from Rome proved to be one of the most important, if not the decisive factor in Poland's survival. Mieszko had three choices open to him: he could remain a pagan, he could enter the eastern Church of Constantinople, as Vladimir the Great did a few years later, or he could turn to Rome. Had he remained a pagan, there is a strong probability that the Poles would have disappeared from the map of Europe, sharing the fate of the western Slavs who lived between the Elbe and the Oder. 'The Slavs are abominable people,' declared the leading princes and bishops of Saxony in a proclamation, 'but their land is very rich in flesh, honey, grain, birds and abounding in all produce of fertility of the earth when cultivated, so that none can compare with it. . . . Wherefore O Saxons, Franks, Lotharingians, men of Flanders most famous, here you can both save your souls and if it please you acquire the best land to live in.'[1] The medieval Germans were not slow to follow this advice and converted the western Slavs by the sword with such thoroughness that the tribes west of the Oder suffered a fate similar to that of the American Red Indians centuries later. Not so the Poles. They and the Christian Czechs (or Bohemians) are the sole survivors of the western Slavs.

The choice of Rome rather than Byzantium was equally fateful, though Mieszko could not have known it. It brought Poland into the mainstream of western culture and turned her into an exposed outpost of Catholicism on the eastern borders of central Europe. When Vladimir the Great embraced the Orthodox branch of Christianity, the two strongest Slav nations, Poland and Russia, were set on their different and frequently colliding courses.

Mieszko received no reward from Rome for bringing Poland

[1] Quoted by H. A. L. Fisher: *A History of Europe*, Arnold, London, 1936.

into the fold. Byzantium proved much more generous to Vladimir the Great, who was canonized in due course, though a less saintly character was difficult to imagine—historians describe him as a fratricide, a monster of cruelty and lust, and credit him with having no fewer than three thousand five hundred concubines.

When Mieszko died in 992, after a less exciting and less sinful life, he left an established country, still a vassal state of the Empire, but well on the way to independence. His son, Boleslas the Brave, was to reach that goal.

By all accounts Boleslas was not a desirable neighbour. He extended the frontiers of his power in all directions and deservedly gained for himself the title of 'our persecutor' given to him in a contemporary Saxon chronicle. Endowed with great charm and a violent temper he was a soldier of genius and a political tactician of no mean order. Under him Poland, still a primitive, illiterate, underpopulated and underdeveloped country which had only just emerged from obscurity, suddenly became a European power feared by all her neighbours.

At first Boleslas seemed content to remain a vassal of the Emperor; he even helped the Germans in a military expedition against a pagan Slav tribe. But the aim of independence and power must have been there from the start. The religious mysticism and romantic outlook of his young contemporary, Emperor Otto III, helped Boleslas to achieve some of his ambitions. Otto was a spiritual follower of Adalbert, the bishop of Prague, who had met a martyr's death during a mission to the pagan Prussians, Poland's northern neighbours. Boleslas had Adalbert's body brought to Gniezno and buried in the Cathedral there. Soon Adalbert was canonized and his shrine in Gniezno became a centre of pilgrimage.

Boleslas, never slow to grasp an opportunity, persuaded both the Pope and the Emperor that the time had come to promote the diocese of Gniezno to the status of an archbishopric. This made the Church in Poland independent of the German ecclesiastical hierarchy, putting it in direct relationship with Rome. To this day Gniezno remains the see of the Primate of Poland.

In the year 1000 Boleslas organized a pilgrimage to St. Adalbert's shrine to coincide with the celebrations accompanying the establishment of the archbishopric. Emperor Otto came in the company of Papal legates and was royally entertained. During a banquet at Gniezno, Otto placed a crown on Boleslas's head and addressed him as 'brother and friend, ally of the Roman people'. Was this the final recognition of Polish sovereignty? Boleslas thought so and tried to confirm it by having himself formally crowned. This required the Pope's permission and envoys were sent to Rome with orders to secure it. Before Boleslas's wish could be granted Otto III died and German opposition frustrated the move. Boleslas had to wait nearly a quarter of a century, but he did not wait idly.

Between 1002 and 1018 Boleslas made his power felt far and wide. He invaded and occupied the eastern mark of Lusatia between the Elbe and the Oder, took over the throne of Bohemia and did his best to oppose every step made by Otto's successor, Henry II. A fifteen years' war with the Empire followed, punctuated by two peace treaties, both of them broken by Boleslas, who on one occasion penetrated to the gates of Magdeburg, plundering everything on his way. During the last stages of the war with Boleslas, the Emperor entered into an alliance with the Russians and in 1017 Poland was attacked from both sides. Boleslas's military genius proved equal to the occasion and for the first and last time in her history Poland was able to defeat a full scale simultaneous attack from east and west. At last, no doubt exhausted by the long struggle, Boleslas and Henry signed yet another peace treaty in which the Germans undertook to send a contingent to help in a Polish campaign against Russia. Immediately Boleslas attacked the Russians and after a short, spectacular campaign entered Kiev where he restored the throne to his son-in-law.

At this stage detailed information about Boleslas's activities ceases abruptly because of the death of our main source, the bishop of Merseburg, Thietmar, who devoted a substantial part of his chronicle to the deeds of the Polish persecutor of the Germans. We know, however, that when the death of Henry II plunged Germany into a crisis, the Pope conceded Boleslas's wish and agreed to his coronation. This duly took place in Gniezno on Christmas Day in the year 1024. Poland was now a sovereign state.

Boleslas died a year later and it is doubtful if there were many mourners in Germany. With his death the first heroic period in Polish history ended as abruptly as it had started. A decline set in during the next three reigns and before the century was out Poland had ceased to be a unified, independent country, becoming a mosaic of duchies and principalities ruled by the numerous descendants of Mieszko I. The fragmented country, torn by dynastic intrigue and civil war, easily fell prey to successive invasions by the Germans, Bohemians and Mongols. More than two centuries passed before another king of Poland was crowned in Cracow, the country's second capital. But the vision of Boleslas the Brave survived and continued to haunt Polish rulers right up to the twentieth century—the vision of a great power, capable of standing up to Russia and Germany simultaneously.

2

THE GREATNESS OF CASIMIR THE GREAT

Cracow, the charming if somewhat sleepy former capital of Poland, is a compulsory stop for every foreign visitor touring the country. And no stay in Cracow, however short, would be complete without a visit to Wawel Hill. There, overlooking the ancient city, a royal castle and a cathedral stand shoulder to shoulder, their buttressed walls almost touching—they are the Westminster Abbey and the Windsor Castle of the former kingdom.

From Wawel Castle the kings of the Piast and Jagellonian dynasties (eleventh to seventeenth centuries) ruled their vast domains and, as the wealth and power of the country grew and the arts flourished, they transformed the old defensive stronghold into a magnificent Renaissance palace, one of the noblest royal residences of the time.

In the Cathedral, kings were crowned and buried during seven centuries, and the heroes of the nation laid to rest even after the capital moved to Warsaw. Visitors can admire their richly carved sarcophagi and in the stillness of the church ponder over Poland's dramatic past. But more conspicuous than any monarch's tomb, occupying the very centre of the main nave, is the shrine of St. Stanislas, a baroque silver casket supported by four angels kneeling on pink marble.

The present communist rulers of Poland do not like being reminded of the significance of this shrine for it commemorates the one occasion when the monarchy clashed head on with the Church and it was the Church who won in the end. King Boleslas the Bold (1058–81) resembled in many ways his illustrious great grandfather whose name he bore. He, too, successfully pursued a great power policy, but his reign ended in sudden disaster. In 1079 Stanislas, the Bishop of Cracow, was accused of treason, tried by a Royal court, sentenced to the loss of limbs, and executed. What exactly was at issue will probably never be known, but the fact remains that the King had asserted his authority over the Bishop. It turned out to be a phyrric victory. Within a year or two Boleslas was forced to flee the country and died in exile. Stanislas was canonized and his shrine occupies the most prominent place in the Wawel cathedral.

Much less conspicuous, hiding at the back of the right aisle of the cathedral, is the tomb of Casimir, the only king in Polish history who has been given the name of Great. On top of the sarcophagus lies a statue of Casimir carved in red Hungarian marble shortly after the monarch's death in 1370. The king has a crown on his head, an orb in his right and a sword in his left hand. Can this conventional rendering tell us anything about the personality of the outstanding ruler of Poland?

The head of the statue is worthy of closer study. Long hair flows in tidy curls from under the royal crown. A high forehead, a firm, straight nose, deeply hooded eyes; a patriarchal beard, also neatly curled, covers the lower part of the face, hiding perhaps a strong chin. Frozen on the slightly parted lips is a smile of worldly wisdom and understanding. The whole impression is of order and benevolence, some vanity perhaps, almost certainly cunning. But has the medieval sculptor done justice to Poland's greatest king?

Outside Poland few people who are not professional historians have even heard of Casimir the Great. He was not a warrior and stands outside the mainstream of Poland's heroic tradition, but he represents solid achievement of the kind which has been rare in Polish history. H. A. L. Fisher in his history of Europe gave Casimir exactly one sentence. Referring to the persecution of the Jews in Rheinish cities and the fact that they found asylum in Poland, he wrote: 'Casimir the Great took occasion to renew the protection which a predecessor had accorded to this community . . . and the high proportion of Semites in modern Poland is not a little due to his enlightened policy, pursued at a moment when no western Jew was safe from the fury of Catholic mobs.'[1]

Had this been Casimir's main or only claim to fame it is certain that the Poles who, on the whole, do not love the Jews, would have never called him Great. His religious tolerance is

[1] *A History of Europe*, p. 319.

only a pointer to the policies and achievements which gave Casimir his unique place in Polish history.

On the whole the best-known and the most admired kings of Poland were warriors: Boleslas the Brave who advanced victoriously to the gates of Magdeburg in the west and Kiev in the east, Ladislas Jagiello who defeated the armed might of the Teutonic Order, Stephen Batory who thrashed the armies of Ivan the Terrible, and John Sobieski who rescued Vienna from the Turks. Casimir had no such military triumphs to his credit. True, he did fight two wars during his thirty-seven years long rule and fought them successfully, but how many monarchs of his day had so little recourse to arms?

Casimir preferred diplomacy and patient treaty to the use of force, especially when he knew that the odds were against him. He was a realist *par excellence*, a superb administrator, firm yet tolerant, a wise legislator, patron of the arts and learning. In short he displayed the characteristics that have been lacking in most of Poland's rulers.

According to a popular saying Casimir found Poland built of wood and left it built of stone. This is true but more in the symbolic than in the literal sense. When in 1333 he came to the throne at the age of only twenty-three Poland was a weak, poor and backward country, only recently reunited by Casimir's father after more than two centuries of fragmentation, internal strife and devastating foreign invasions. There was no effective central administration, no coherent system of law and only the personality of the king seemed to stand between the country and renewed chaos. Important provinces had been lost in the south-east, the south-west and in the north, cutting the country off from the Baltic. And while Poland had grown weaker, her neighbours had grown stronger, laying claims to more land, and even to the crown itself. Most menacing of all, an aggressive new power had appeared on Poland's northern flank—the Order of the Teutonic Knights.

Twenty years after his accession, Casimir played host in Cracow to a glittering European assembly: Emperor Charles IV (who had married Casimir's granddaughter), the King of Hungary (Casimir's chief ally and brother-in-law), the King of Denmark (Casimir's latest ally), the King of Cyprus, and a host of princes and ambassadors. On the agenda: a new Crusade, the eastern question, and a dispute between Hungary and the Empire with Casimir acting as arbitrator.

While the royal guests were being lavishly entertained by their host and the burghers of Cracow, a new university founded by Casimir in that city was opening its doors—the second university to be created outside England and the Latin countries. Suddenly Poland was again a European power.

Casimir achieved the miracle almost entirely by pacific means. Patiently, step by step, he consolidated his kingdom, putting an end to regional anarchy, introducing efficient central administration, fair justice and sound laws. He built new cities and developed old ones, letting them flourish on international trade. He stimulated land settlement, protected the peasants from harsh exploitation and supplied them from State granaries when the harvest was bad. Education received strong encouragement under his reign and the foundation of the University of Cracow was the most striking example of progress achieved. Altogether under his wise, benevolent, yet firm, rule Poland made greater strides in two decades than in the preceeding four centuries.

In foreign policy Casimir relied on diplomatic skill, patience, persuasion and, in the last resort, money. He never gave up Poland's claims to Silesia and Pomerania, the provinces that had been lost to Bohemia and the Teutonic Knights respectively, but he did not press the claims to the point of war knowing full well that he had little chance of winning in battle. He was even prepared to pay handsomely for what he could not obtain by diplomacy and handed over a large sum of money to the King of Bohemia in return for the latter surrendering his claim to the crown of Poland. In his dispute with the Teutonic Knights, Casimir tried to obtain justice in a canonical court. When the Court's findings favourable to Poland were set aside, he entered into direct negotiations with the Knights and managed to gain some territorial concessions.

Only in the east, where no superior military power confronted him, did Casimir go to war. It appears that he inherited from a relative the title to the duchy of Halicz and Volhynia on the south-eastern borders of his kingdom (now a part of Western Ukraine) but his claim was contested by the rulers of Lithuania. Casimir fought two campaigns and in the end not only held on to the disputed duchy but also to the adjoining province of Podole, extending Polish frontiers further east than ever before.

These newly acquired lands were not ethnically Polish, their population was mainly Ruthenian and belonged to the Orthodox Rite. Casimir's policy towards his new subjects was sensible and moderate. He allowed a good measure of local autonomy and introduced religious freedom; though he supported the spread of Roman Catholicism he also took steps to strengthen the organization of the Orthodox Church.

Communist historians reproach Casimir for not having made greater efforts to regain Silesia and Pomerania and for expanding eastward instead. It must be for them a source of embarrassment to have the example of Poland's undisputedly greatest king pursuing a policy which has been violently contradicted by Stalin's brutal redrawing of Polish frontiers. But the argument about the rights and wrongs of Casimir's eastern policy is academic. The important thing is that his acquisition of the vast tracts of what now is western Ukraine, inaugurated an entirely new phase in Poland's history; Casimir, the realist, laid the foundations for what was to become the vast Polish commonwealth, which eventually stretched from the Baltic to the Black Sea, embracing half a dozen nations. This commonwealth led to Poland's greatest triumphs. It also brought disasters and untold miseries, for many of Casimir's successors lacked not only his ability but above all his wisdom and tolerance.

3

THE TEUTONIC KNIGHTS

Ten years after King John reluctantly signed the Magna Carta, a Polish prince with apparent eagerness put his name to a document which has had a much less beneficial but more dramatic influence on the history of Europe. The Prince, Conrad of Mazovia, invited the Teutonic Knights into his duchy, opened the door to Prussian expansion on the Baltic and unwittingly helped to lay the foundations of the aggressive Kingdom of Prussia.

Conrad was a direct descendant of Boleslas the Brave but inherited none of his ancestor's genius; he was a mediocre and ignorant man, ill-versed in matters of diplomacy, uninformed about the outside world. He fell for what seemed to him a simple solution to a simple problem. Mazovia, the north-eastern of the several duchies into which Poland had disintegrated towards the end of the eleventh century, had troublesome neighbours in the Prussians who lived between Conrad's duchy and the Baltic Sea. Apart from their name and their aggressiveness they had nothing in common with the Prussians of Frederick the Great; they were a fierce Baltic tribe, related to the Lithuanians, Letts and Estonians. Not only had they resisted two centuries of efforts to convert them to Christianity, but they made life very difficult for Conrad and his subjects by constant raids into Poland across the 150 miles long frontier with Mazovia, ravaging the countryside and repeatedly burning down Conrad's capital.

Too weak to deal with the situation himself, Conrad accepted a suggestion which must have appeared to him irresistibly attractive: invite the Teutonic Knights to settle in his frontier area and from there engage in the good work of converting and subduing the troublesome Prussians while protecting Mazovia; of course, the Knights would be Conrad's subjects and by their missionary and military activities extend his realm into the

Prussian lands. The Teutonic Knights accepted Conrad's invitation, but they had their own ideas about the future.

Had Conrad made inquiries about the Order, he might have had second thoughts. Originally set up in Syria in 1190 under the innocuous name of *Ordo militium hospitalis S. Mariae Teutonicorum Hierosolymitami*, with the object of supporting the German hospital and organizing German crusades in the Holy Land, it discovered that activities nearer home were more profitable. In 1224 the Order (also known as the Crutched Knights or Order of the Cross) was expelled by King Andrew of Hungary when he found that the Knights were trying to set up a state of their own in the part of Transylvania where he had settled them. But it seems that Conrad was unaware of this ominous incident and to him the proposition of inviting the Order seemed safe and sensible. He gave them the land of Chelmno as their base.

Thus Conrad altered the future not only of Poland but of the whole of Europe. The events that followed his fatal invitation to the Teutonic Knights have had a traumatic and lasting impact on the national consciousness of the Poles.

The Knights moved in between 1226 and 1230 and in less than a century they not only conquered the whole of Prussia but also Polish Pomerania, thus cutting off Poland from the sea. In Prussia the native pagans were either killed or forcibly converted to Christianity and a period of intensive German colonization followed along the whole of Poland's northern flank. The Teutonic Order, called in by Conrad to protect him from the Prussians, soon became the most menacing of Poland's neighbours and the seeds of future disasters, right down to the twentieth century, were well and truly sown.

How did a numerically small Order achieve such power in a relatively short time? The answer lies in their superior civil and military administration, combined with ruthless fighting methods and an utterly unscrupulous diplomacy. Before the ink was dry on Conrad's invitation, and without his knowledge, the Grand Master of the Teutonic Knights obtained from Emperor Frederick II confirmation of their rights to the Polish land of Chelmno, the outright grant of the whole of Prussia, and for himself and his successors the status of Princes of the Empire. This was the first of several such acts in the tangled history of the Order's relations with Poland. The second came eight years later when the Knights presented the Pope with a falsified text of the privilege granted to them by Conrad. According to the forged version the Polish Prince had given them 'full sovereignty in the lands of Chelmno and Prussia'. On this basis the Knights induced the Holy See to transfer to the Order the stewardship of those territories, declaring them the 'property of St. Peter'. Having thus obtained both the Emperor's and the Pope's blessing for the annexation of their first base, the Knights proceeded to extend the conquest both in the easterly and in the westerly direction and succeeded in occupying the whole of Polish Pomerania.

When Poland was reunited at the beginning of the fourteenth century almost the first act of the newly crowned king, Ladislas Lokietek, was to start a legal process against the Order's annexation of Pomerania. Judges appointed by the Pope sat for a whole year taking evidence from scores of witnesses and in 1321 they pronounced in Poland's favour; the Knights were ordered to return eastern Pomerania and to pay the King 30,000 pieces of silver in compensation. The Order lodged an appeal and the judgment was never executed. War followed, but Poland was not strong enough to defeat the Order.

Casimir the Great also tried to regain Pomerania by taking the Order to court, but once more the Knights managed to get the judgment set aside and the Polish King did not feel strong enough to pursue his claim by force. Only when the Poles joined hands with the Lithuanians under Ladislas Jagiello were they in a position to challenge the might of the Order.

In 1410, near the village of Grunwald (Tannenberg), their combined forces confronted the armies of the Teutonic Knights. Chanting the ancient Polish hymn: 'Virgin Mother of God, Blessed be the Lord. Mary! Mary!', Jagiello's hosts struck and inflicted a crushing defeat on the Order. But even then the issue was not yet decided. Only half a century later, after a thirteen years' war, did Poland regain Pomerania, and Prussia formally became a fief of the Polish Crown in 1466.

This was the beginning of a new and odd chapter. The Grand Masters of the Teutonic Order, though owing allegiance to the King, continued to plot against him with the view of regaining Pomerania and joining the Empire. This led to another inconclusive war (1519–21). Four years after its end the Order performed an astonishing volte-face: the Grand Master approached Sigismund I for permission to securalize the Order and to embrace Lutheranism. The Polish King, though a pious Catholic himself, agreed to the proposal hoping no doubt that the change would at least prevent the Order from further plotting with the Catholic Empire and the Vatican against the interests of Poland.

On 10th April 1525, in the great square in Cracow, Albrecht von Hohenzollern, the former Grand Master, now a hereditary Duke of Prussia, solemnly paid homage to Sigismund I. From now on he and his heirs were entitled to a seat in the Polish Senate; the Catholic Kings of Poland not only had a German province, but a Protestant one at that. In the tolerant climate of that century in Poland, when the country was at the peak of its power, the arrangement worked reasonably well, with one branch of the Hohenzollerns ruling in Brandenburg as hereditary electors of the Empire and the other in East Prussia as vassals of Poland.

But in the middle of the next century, when Poland found herself at the nadir of her fortunes, invaded by the Swedes, Russians, Cossacks, Tartars and Transylvanians, in return for a promise of help from the Elector, King John Casimir ceded East Prussia to him (1657). It was not very long before the Elector's son, Frederick I, proclaimed himself King of Prussia (1701) and during the century that followed Poland disappeared from the map, divided between Prussia, Austria and Russia.

To this day the struggle against the Teutonic Knights is a part of the atavistic memories of every Pole. Novels, paintings and films still remind him of this now remote chapter of history. Henryk Sienkiewicz (who won a Nobel Prize for his *Quo Vadis?*) wrote a long and gory novel about the Knights, culminating in an ecstatic description of their defeat at Grunwald. A film of this novel was made just in time for the millennium celebrations. Poland's leading historical painter, Jan Matejko, devoted one enormous canvas to the Battle of Grunwald and another to Albert's homage in Cracow.

On the occasion of the fifth centenary of Grunwald in 1910 the Poles erected in Cracow a hideous monument (a gift to the city from the famous pianist, Paderewski): an overpowering plinth of roughly hewn granite surrounded by symbolic figures in bronze and crowned with a huge equestrian statue of Ladislas Jagiello. During the Second World War, the Grunwald monument was among the first to be deliberately destroyed by the Germans. To its credit, the Communist Government of post-war Poland did not have it rebuilt (though it put a picture of it on postage stamps); instead they had a new one, in modern style, built on the site of the battle itself at Grunwald, which is now once more within the frontiers of Poland.

Why this cult of Grunwald? An official Polish publication states: 'We see in this battle a symbol of the defence of the native land and of the rights of every nation to a free, sovereign development.' Fair enough, but there is more to it. The story of the Teutonic Knights illustrates vividly the German danger to Poland and that danger causes recurring nightmares not only to the Warsaw politicians, but to every Pole. For very good historical reasons the Poles are afraid of Germany and it is in the interest of the present Government in Warsaw that they should remain so. At the same time it is essential for the morale of the nation to keep on reminding people that there was a time, even if it happened as long as five centuries ago, when Poland conquered the Teutonic menace.

4

POLAND'S COMMONWEALTH

It has been said that England acquired her Empire in a fit of absentmindedness; Poland obtained hers through the most sensational and unromantic royal marriage of the fourteenth century.

The native Piast dynasty, which had ruled the country for four hundred years, came to an end when Casimir the Great died without issue (1370). His nephew, Louis the Great of Hungary, inherited the Polish throne and reigned over the two countries for a dozen years—not a very happy period for Poland. Determined to have a monarch of their own, the Polish nobles agreed with Louis that on his death one of his three daughters should succeed to the Cracow throne. When Louis died his youngest daughter, Jadwiga, was named Queen of Poland.

There was, however, one serious snag: Jadwiga, though not yet ten years old, was already married. When she was only five her father had arranged her wedding to William von Hapsburg, though according to canon law the marriage would become void unless consummated when she reached the age of thirteen. This gave the Polish nobles a chance to put into operation their own plan of action. They were almost united in not wanting to see a German prince on the throne and thought that Ladislas Jagiello, the Grand Duke of Lithuania, would be a much better choice. Secret negotiations with him started in 1383.

Jadwiga, oblivious of what was in store for her, arrived in Cracow and was crowned in 1384. She still fondly imagined that William Hapsburg, her friend and childhood companion, would soon join her as husband and consort. When the envoys of Jagiello presented themselves at Wawel Castle and formally asked for her hand on behalf of their master, Jadwiga was incredulous and refused to take the proposal seriously.

Her reaction was understandable, for a more incongruous

match was difficult to imagine. Jadwiga was still a child, Jagiello was thirty-six; she was a devout Catholic, he was a pagan; she had been brought up at one of the most splendid and sophisticated courts of Europe, he seemed to be practically a barbarian. Yet the Polish nobles were not acting just out of a perverse desire to make their Queen unhappy; they had solid reasons of state for wishing her to marry the Grand Duke of Lithuania.

Poland and Lithuania had a long common frontier and one common enemy—the Teutonic Knights, who were threatening the very existence of both states; at the same time they were both interested in eastward expansion and this had repeatedly brought them into conflict with each other. Divided they were bound to fall to the Knights, united they would become one of the greatest powers of Europe. Indeed the young Grand Duchy of Lithuania had expanded eastward so fast that it was already larger than Poland.

But Lithuania was also the last pagan state in Europe, at least the Lithuanians themselves were largely pagans and they alone among the Baltic peoples had resisted the crusading and conquering attempts of the Teutonic Knights. However, their own conquests had brought under their rule large numbers of eastern Slavs who worshipped in the Greek Orthodox Church. Thus a union with Poland, if accompanied by a baptism of the Grand Duke and his pagan subjects, offered the prospect of extending the influence of the Roman Church while removing the main pretext for the Teutonic Knights' interest in Lithuania.

The mutual advantages were clear. From Jagiello's point of view there was also the additional attraction of the Polish crown helping to strengthen his own position inside Lithuania, where it was constantly threatened by his ambitious cousin. Without much hesitation he signed an agreement with the Polish nobles undertaking to accept the Roman Catholic faith (together with those of his subjects who were pagans) in return for Jadwiga's hand and the crown of Poland.

But Jadwiga was still not willing to marry Jagiello. For six long months she resisted the arguments and the pressure of her advisers. In the end, however, the religious argument prevailed; she agreed to make a personal sacrifice for the sake of the

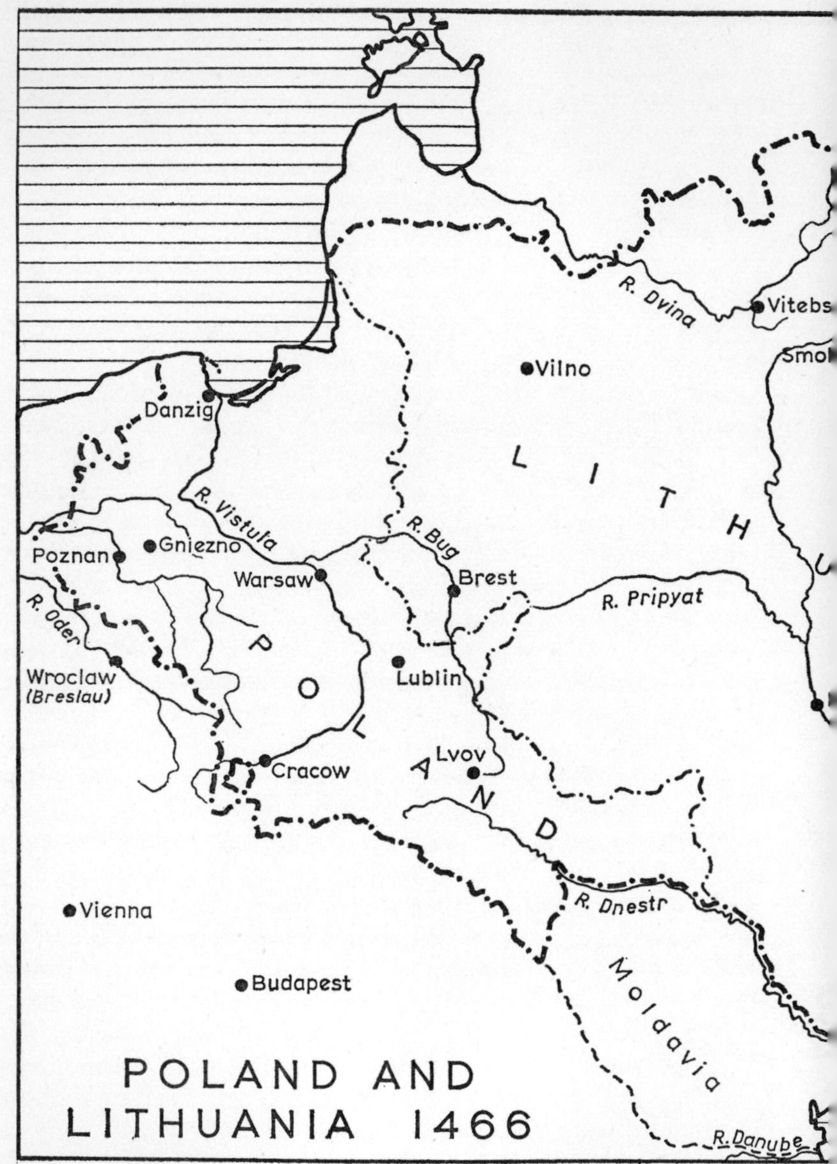
R. Dvina
Vitebs
Smol
Vilno
Danzig
L I T H U
R. Vistula
R. Bug
Gniezno
Poznan
Warsaw
Brest
R. Pripyat
R. Oder
P O L A N D
Wroclaw
(Breslau)
Lublin
Lvov
Cracow
R. Dnestr
Vienna
Moldavia
Budapest
R. Danube
POLAND AND
LITHUANIA 1466

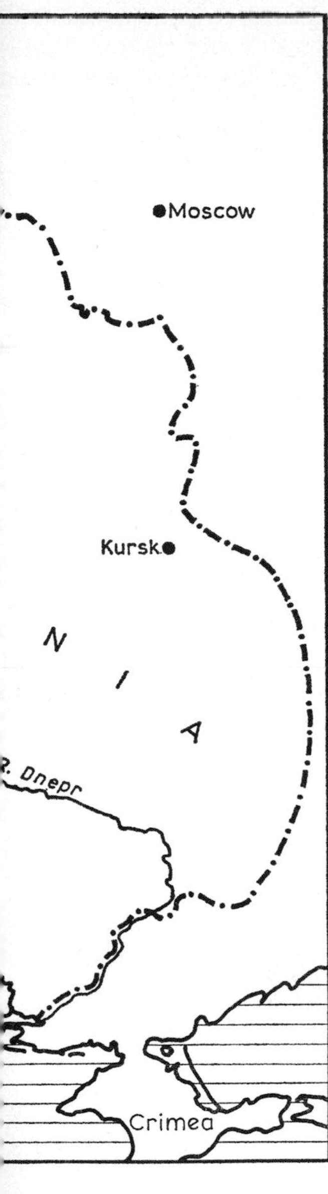

3

Church, which saw in this marriage a golden opportunity for winning many souls and much influence.

When the news of Jadwiga's reluctant agreement reached him, Jagiello was engaged in yet another war with the Teutonic Knights, but without waiting to finish it he hurried to Poland as Jadwiga's thirteenth birthday approached. In quick succession he was baptized, married to the Polish Queen and crowned in the Wawel Cathedral (1386).

The marriage of Jadwiga and Jagiello inaugurated the era of Poland's imperial expansion and gave the country the security it so badly needed. The combined forces of Poland and Lithuania were strong enough to take on any adversary. In 1410 they inflicted a crushing defeat on the Teutonic Order and the Crutched Knights ceased to be a serious threat to the existence of the united Kingdom.

What might have been an ephemeral link between two countries under a common ruler gradually, though not without difficulty, became a permanent union. In 1569 in the city of Lublin, near the Polish-Lithuanian frontier, the assembled spiritual and temporal lords, the joint Councils of State and the deputies of the gentry of both countries signed the final Act of Union, declaring: 'The kingdom of Poland and the Grand Duchy of Lithuania have become one organic and indivisible body and also one equal and joint Commonwealth, in which the two States and nations have joined and fused together. . . .'

This Union survived the dynasty of Jagiello and a succession of elected kings right to the partitions of Poland at the end of the eighteenth century. The idea of the Polish-Lithuanian Commonwealth, comprising the lands of White Russia and the Ukraine, survived in Polish minds much longer, to the present day. Between 1569 and 1945 that idea, sometimes combined with visions of even greater expansion to the east, brought Poland repeatedly into conflict with Russian imperialism. It took the ruthless power of Stalin to remove it completely from the realm of practical politics.

But these dangers were in the future. While the Jagiellonian dynasty ruled from Cracow, the United Kingdom enjoyed its golden age; Poland and Lithuania had everything they needed: power, security and prosperity. Doors were wide open to ideas from the West; the sciences and the arts flourished. Humanism and the Renaissance made a profound impression on Polish minds and left magnificent examples of art and architecture. The winds of the Reformation blew across the Polish plain, achieving a good many converts, but provoking practically no persecution. It was a happy country indeed.

Lithuania and the vast lands in the east had a large measure of autonomy. Lithuanian nobility and gentry enjoyed the same rights and privileges as their Polish counterparts and in both countries they formed a large class, probably comprising a tenth of the population, including at one end of the spectrum the magnates, like the Radziwills, whose lands were vaster than the whole of Belgium, and at the other the small country gentry, some of whom owned perhaps only as little as a few score of acres.

While constitutionally the two countries of the Commonwealth were equals, there could be no doubt as to where the centre of gravity lay. Cracow, with its glittering Royal court in the splendid Renaissance castle and the university reformed by Jagiello, was an irresistible magnet; from there radiated Polish culture and civilization. In Lithuania the nobility and the gentry became gradually Polonized of their own free will and they became indistinguishable from the Poles. Several centuries later the greatest Polish poet, Adam Mickiewicz, wrote:

Oh Lithuania,
My fatherland, thou are like good health.
How much to prize thee can only be told
By him who has lost thee. . . .

But he wrote this in Polish, regarded himself as a Pole and Lithuania as a part of Poland. Paderewski, the famous pianist and statesman, and Marshal Joseph Pilsudski, who shaped the destinies of Poland between the two world wars, were also members of the Lithuanian gentry, yet Poles to the core.

As stated in the Act of the Lublin Union the two nations had indeed become one, or so it seemed on the surface. And a similar process was under way in the vast tracts of White Russia and the Ukraine. But the process of peaceful, spontaneous Polonization did not touch the peasantry. The peasants still spoke their native tongues, Lithuanian, Latvian, White Russian and Ukrainian, and remained largely unaffected by what was happening to the gentry; this was the seed of disasters to come. However, at that time Moscow had not yet emerged as a centre of great power and Russia, divided into warring duchies, was still groaning under the Tartar yoke; nobody in Poland was worried about dangers on that front. Ivan the Great had not yet been born; Peter the Great was still centuries away. The Polish-Lithuanian state seemed to have the security of vastness, with its frontiers stretching from a hundred miles to the west of Moscow to a similar distance to the east of Berlin, from the Baltic in the north to the Black Sea in the south. Most of this empire Poland had acquired not by conquest, but by Jagiello's marriage to Jadwiga. In fact, wars of conquest were never Poland's speciality. The country was simply not geared to sustained military effort and there was enough trouble with aggressive neighbours to absorb any warlike energies of the nation.

If the period of Jagiellonian rule (1386–1572) has been described as Poland's golden age, it was not because of victories of the sword, but because of prosperity and the flowering of the arts and of political and scientific thought. The most outstanding feature of that period was the spirit of tolerance and freedom, which contrasted sharply with conditions in most European countries. Already at the Council of Constance (1415) the Ambassador of Ladislas Jagiello, Paul Wlodkowicz, argued eloquently:

One must not harass either the persons or the property of the infidel who wish to live in peace among Christians. . . . Therefore a ruler who deprives them of their fortune without cause commits a sin, for not even the Pope is allowed to do this. . . . And the greatest tolerance is due to the Jews, because we use their Books to prove the correctness of our truth and our faith. . . .

. . . the infidel must not be deprived of their property or their offices, because they possess these by the will of the Lord. . . . This conclusion is based on the Book of Exodus, Chapter 20: 'Thou shalt not kill. Thou shalt not steal'. These words forbid all robbery and violence.

The question is asked: can the property of heretics or schismatics be seized? I think not, and for the same reasons that apply to the infidel.

The infidel must not be compelled to accept the Christian faith by force of arms or oppression, because this would mean inflicting a wrong on our fellow men, and because wrong should not be done to achieve good. . . . Nobody must be compelled to believe, for faith cannot result from compulsion and extorted prayers are not pleasing to the Lord. . . .

These words were spoken on 5th July 1415. Even allowing for the fact that the Polish argument was directed against the ruthless methods of the Teutonic Knights, it remains a remarkable formulation of the thesis of tolerance. Nor was it just a theoretical statement of principles—the actual practice under Jagiellonian kings was by and large based on these principles. And when the last of the dynasty died in 1572 and Polish-Lithuanian nobles and gentry assembled in Warsaw to elect his successor, they drew up an act which has gone down in history as the Warsaw Confederation. It was signed by all the lay members of the Diet and the Senate, but by only one bishop. The document read:

. . . Since there is no little disagreement in our Commonwealth in matters of Christian Religion, in order to prevent this leading to internal strife, which we can clearly observe in other Kingdoms, we promise each other on our own and our descentants' behalf for ever and ever, under oath on our Faith, Honour and Conscience. . . . to keep the peace among ourselves and not to shed blood for differences in religion or church observance, or punish each other by seizure of property, prison or exile. . . .

Hand in hand with religious tolerance went political freedom.

In 1430 Ladislas Jagiello, in the *Neminem Captivabimus* privilege, gave the gentry freedom from arrest and punishment except by a due process of law. Seventy years later his grandson, Alexander, signed the *Nihil novi* statutes:

> Since common laws and public constitutions concern not one person but the whole nation, we have decreed that from now and for ever thereafter nothing new shall be decreed by us or our successors without the joint consent of the Lords of the Council and the Deputies from the constituencies. . . .

In the turbulent and intolerant Europe of the fifteenth and sixteenth centuries Poland was indeed a haven of freedom and peaceful tolerance. But was the ruling class mature enough to profit from that freedom? The next two centuries showed that it was not. Abused freedom turned into licence and anarchy. The writing was already on the walls of the Jagiellonian commonwealth, but there were few wise enough to decipher it.

PART TWO

DECLINE AND FALL

5

'EQUALS OF THE KING'

Father Stanislas Orzechowski, a sixteenth-century Polish priest of noble birth was one of the great European eccentrics. He epitomized some of the best and some of the worst in Polish character; unwittingly he affected the fate of his country. Yet, strangely enough he is practically unknown even in Poland.

He was probably better educated than any of his contemporaries. As a young man he studied in Vienna, Wittenberg (where he came under the influence of Luther), Padua, Bologna and finally Rome, where he turned to fanatical Catholicism. On his return to Poland, writing in impeccable, Ciceronian Latin, he thundered against the Protestants and called for a crusade against the Turks. On one point, however, he deviated from the teachings of his Church: he was against the celibacy of the clergy. In pressing this point he did not satisfy himself with eloquent writings but translated them into deeds. First he officiated at the marriage of a fellow Catholic priest, then he declared publicly that he would himself enter into matrimony, and finally he did so. At last the patience of his superiors was exhausted. By a sentence of a bishop's Court he was excommunicated, deprived of all rights and property, and banished from the country.

Orzechowski appealed to the gentry for support and found it readily forthcoming, because the financial and legal privileges of the Church were strongly resented. The Diet of 1552 decreed that civil authorities should suspend for the period of one year the execution of judgments passed by ecclesiastical courts. This was meant to be a temporary expedient, but it became a permanent feature of the Polish system; the power of the bishops was broken to the premature joy of all the Protestants.

Even though excommunicated, Orzechowski remained faithful to Rome in his own individualistic way. He continued to fulminate against heresy and demand that the power of the

Church, which he himself had defied, should always be supreme. At the same time he extolled the virtues of the system based on the liberties of the gentry. He wrote with pride:

'Consider the Pole's position in the world, proud in his freedom, resplendent in his liberties, dressed in the glorious robe of rights equal with those of the King; that is why the Pole wears the fine, gold ring of nobility, which makes equals of the highest and the lowest in the land.'

For Orzechowski the term 'Pole' meant a member of the gentry or nobility; like many of his contemporaries he equated the nation with the ruling class. In fact the ruling class was divided into two very unequal groups which in theory at least enjoyed exactly the same legal status. The apex of the social pyramid was occupied by a few score of great landowning families, whose estates were often in the Grand Duchy of Lithuania and in the eastern provinces. Their wealth was fabulous. While in other countries the great landowners measured their estates in tens or hundreds of thousands of acres, in Poland, if they knew their approximate size, they expressed it in millions. The Princes Ostrogski, for instance, had about one hundred towns and castles and some twelve hundred villages on their land, which brought them an income bigger than the State revenue. And vast fortunes were still being made in the service of the Crown; the brilliant Chancellor and Commander-in-Chief, John Zamoyski, started modestly as the owner of a few villages, but the generosity of two successive monarchs increased his property to two hundred villages on land twice the size of the State of Rhode Island or more than three times the size of Oxfordshire. In addition he had been given twice that amount of land for life.

By custom most of the great offices of State, provincial and county governorships went to members of the wealthy landed families. Since many of the Roman Catholic bishops were also members of these families, the rich nobles dominated the Senate by virtue of holding the high, civil, military and spiritual appointments which entitled them to a seat in the Upper Chamber. The nobles lived in truly royal style in their castles and palaces, maintaining private armies often larger than the minute standing army of the King.

Constitutionally there was no dividing line between those

princely families and the great masses of the gentry who numbered hundreds of thousands. The gentry had full political rights and they formed the nation about which Orzechowski wrote with such rapture. They elected the national and provincial Diets, they carried arms and served in the Army, they had the right to hold offices under the Crown. Many of them were relatively impecunious, owning only a farm or two, the majority were squires of one or more villages.

Though the gentry and the great nobles formed together the ruling class of Poland, their interests were not always indentical and the gentry viewed the nobles with suspicion, jealously guarding its rights and privileges against any attempt to increase the powers of the King or the Senate. The remaining two classes had no political influence. The wealthier of the town dwellers represented an insignificant middle class. They were largely German immigrants, settled in cities under the Magdeburg law, preserving their German institutions, though in Cracow and most other big cities they became gradually Polonized and, even in Gdansk, where they remained thoroughly German, they were intensely loyal to Poland and fought the Teutonic Knights with fervour and success. Also in the cities there were large numbers of Jews living under their own laws, but with no political rights whatsoever.

Finally the great masses of peasantry, who tilled the soil of the gentry, were at the mercy of their masters and not allowed to leave the land. The gentry were not only their employers but also the judges of the peasants and they exacted from them an increasing amount of servitude.

Thus Poland was socially and politically divided into three nations, if not four. The wealth and influence were in the hands of the few great nobles, but they had to share their political power with the often impecunious gentry, who had extended and consolidated the rights in the sixteenth century. The powers of the King became strictly limited and the Poles proudly described their country as a Royal Republic.

The Roman Church occupied a privileged position. Its bishops sat in the Senate, and this was not seriously disputed, but the gentry resented strongly the Church's right to impose taxes. This, combined with the individualistic nature of the Poles, made the ideas of the Reformation particularly attractive to them. The teachings of Luther and Calvin appealed to many and Protestant sects proliferated and flourished for a time. During the reign of the last Jagiellonian King, Sigismund Augustus (1520–72), it even looked as if the King himself might break with Rome, but in the event he remained faithful to Catholicism.

The impact of Protestant ideas was greatest among the nobles, the gentry and the town dwellers, but it left the peasants largely unaffected. Strangely enough it was the Orzechowski case, which restricted the power of the Church, that took the wind out of Protestant sails. The gentry, having won its battle against ecclesiastical jurisdiction seemed to lose interest in Protestantism. The divisions among the various Protestant sects on the one hand and the counter-offensive of the Catholic Church led by the Jesuits on the other, did the rest; the number of Protestants began to dwindle and their influence receded.

Even if the Reformation never gained the upper hand in Poland, it made a lasting impact on Polish political thought. Andrew Frycz Modrzewski, the secretary to Sigismund Augustus, was among the leading Protestant writers and thinkers of his time. His great five-volume work entitled *About the Repair of the Republic* (*De republica emendanda*), first published in 1551, presented a complete and coherent survey of all problems facing the state and expressed views far ahead of his time. Frycz Modrzewski advocated, for instance, the emancipation of the peasants and the complete equality of all before the law. 'And should we have any differences in penalties,' he wrote, 'those in high offices should suffer more severe penalties than people of a lower order, the rich should be punished more than the poor. . . .'

A sound economist and a sworn enemy of all unjust laws, Frycz Modrzewski argued that the State should accept the responsibility for the poor; he was also the first writer of his period to favour a general system of State education. His great work, translated into French, German and Spanish, left a mark on European political thought, but his ideas were too revolutionary; it took centuries before they could be put into practice.

In Poland Frycz Modrzewski was not an isolated phenomenon. Eighteen years after the publication of his great work another remarkable political treatise came from the pen of

Lawrence Grzymala Goslicki. It was entitled *De Optimo Senatore* and in the English translation *The Accomplished Senator*. The first two English editions (in 1598 and 1607) were, however, suppressed in England as seditious; his work had to wait nearly two centuries before it could openly reach the English public, though according to some authorities copies of it circulated privately, influencing among others William Shakespeare.

What were the ideas of Goslicki which were regarded as seditious in the England of Elizabeth I and James I? The essence of them was contained in the following passages:

> The well-being and welfare of each State must be measured by the well-being and welfare of its subjects. . . . Kings are made for the good of the nation and not for their own good. . . . They rule under the law through the law; the great task of their Government is to maintain and preserve the laws and the liberties of their people. . . .
>
> Wherever the principle of equality falls into contempt or is badly applied, by the very nature of things internal friction and strife follow . . . with those who are equal striving for a state of inequality and superiority, while those regarded as inferior aim at creating conditions of equality. . . .
>
> It happens that a nation, rightly provoked and angered by tyranny . . . exercises the undeniable right to defend the liberties and either through effective conspiracy or in an open fight throws away the yoke, expels its lords and rulers and takes the government into its own hands. . . .

When Goslicki's book was first published in Poland in 1569, the ideas it contained were largely accepted political thinking and his principles either already had been or were about to be incorporated in the Constitution. In many ways Poland of the sixteenth century seemed to be a model modern constitutional state. Unfortunately the gentry and the nobles allowed the idea of freedom to go to their heads. Frycz Modrzewski saw some of the dangers clearly. 'Oh Lord,' he prayed, 'make all the gentry set aside the love of themselves and love the Commonwealth instead, that is all the people who dwell here, sharing the life of our society; make them care for all and make them defend everybody's life, wealth and virtue!'

Poland had to wait a very long time for this prayer to be

answered. Meanwhile the Polish gentry reigned supreme, intelligent but short-sighted, tolerant towards its members but intolerant to others, individualistic, rebellious, greedy and generous at the same time, above all emotional and anarchic. Long before Louis XIV they proclaimed themselves to be the nation and the state, and proceeded to make the worst of it.

6

'POLAND'S STRENGTH LIES IN ANARCHY'

The slow-motion tragedy of the decline and fall of Poland began to unfold when Sigismund Augustus, the last of the Jagiellons, died in 1572. He left the country at the peak of its power; two centuries of Jagiellonion rule had transformed a medium-sized, essentially one-nation State into a vast Commonwealth of many nations; Poles, Lithuanians, Latvians, Byelorussians, Ukrainians, Germans, Jews and Armenians lived peacefully side by side. There were six official languages: Polish, Latin, Ruthenian, German, Hebrew and Armenian. Roman Catholicism was the religion of the State, but its adherents were probably outnumbered by the Greek Orthodox, Protestants and other minorities. In the Europe torn by intolerance and by dynastic and religious wars Poland stood for freedom, peace, stability and prosperity. What went wrong subsequently?

It would be easy to blame Poland's downfall on bad neighbours. She was indeed very unlucky to find herself surrounded by rapacious, militaristic Prussia, imperialistic Russia and greedy Austria. To survive amidst such neighbours was bound to be difficult, but it was the Poles themselves who made it impossible. Step by step, and with considerable pride, they created a system of government unique in the world, which might have perhaps succeeded in a remote island kingdom protected by the vastness of the sea. But Poland was no island, she even had no natural frontiers to speak of. In her condition the system was guaranteed to lead to calamity.

The three mainsprings of the Polish system of misgovernment were elective monarchy, the *liberum veto* and the legal rebellion. The principle of elective monarchy was by no means a Polish invention. It had been tried elsewhere with bad results, but the Poles managed to give it an even more disastrous twist. On the other hand the *liberum veto* had no parallel in any other country; to find something akin to it we have to go to the

Council of the League of Nations, which operated on the principle of unanimity. The practice of legal rebellion, if not the concept, was also a Polish speciality.

The first ominous signs of trouble appeared during the election of Sigismund Augustus's successor. In theory the monarchy had been elective ever since the days of Ladislas Jagiello, but since the choice of the King was limited in practice to the members of the dynasty, who were the hereditary Grand Dukes of Lithuania, the election was more or less a formality. Now that the dynasty had died out, the choice was wide open and the gentry was determined to have its full say. Since all the members of the gentry and nobility were equally liable to be called to arms, they demanded to have an equal voice in directly choosing the monarch on the principle of one man one vote. This was conceded and nine months after the death of the King, the electors, more than fifty thousand of them, all carrying arms, assembled outside Warsaw to choose the successor.

Those nine months of interregnum had been filled by endless arguments, manœuvres and counter-manœuvres between the still influential Protestants and the increasingly militant Catholics, between the gentry on the one side and the nobles on the other, and between the various factions of the gentry itself. The Protestants had won an important victory in getting the Warsaw Confederation to guarantee religious freedom, the Catholics had scored a success in establishing that the Primate, the Archbishop of Gniezno and not the Grand Marshall, who happened to be a Calvinist, should act as Regent pending the election of a new monarch.

The long delay enabled the various candidates to the throne to engage in electioneering of the worst kind. Their envoys, laden with gold and promises, converged on Warsaw and started distributing their masters' largesse. Five men were competing for the Polish crown: Henri de Valois of France (a younger son of Catherine de Medici), John III of Sweden (a brother-in-law of the last Polish king) and his son Sigismund, the Archduke Ernest of Austria (son of Emperor Maximillian II) and finally Ivan the Terrible of Moscow.

The favourite of the nobles and of the Church was Archduke Ernest, but the gentry adamantly opposed the election of a German prince. The leader of this opposition, John Zamoyski,

Casimir the Great, King of Poland (1333–70), laid the foundations of his country's greatness in the fifteenth and sixteenth centuries. The King's statue carved shortly after his death lies on his tomb in the Wawel Cathedral

On Wawel Hill in Cracow the Cathedral and the Royal Castle stand side by side, their buttressed walls almost touching; they are the Westminster Abbey and the Windsor Castle of Poland

pointed to the example of Bohemia, which had lost all independence under Hapsburg rule. Even more telling was the intervention of the Sultan of Turkey, who let it be known that he would not stand idly by and see a Hapsburg elected to the Polish throne. . . .

The two Swedish candidates commanded little support for they had little to offer. The Lithuanian gentry favoured Ivan the Terrible in the hope that his election would bring peace with Moscow and also that he would break the power of the nobles as he had done in Russia. However, when Ivan's conditions became known (hereditary monarchy, his coronation according to the Orthodox rite and the transfer of Kiev to Russia) support for him soon evaporated.

This left the field to Henri de Valois, who appealed to the Catholics, but was firmly opposed by the Protestants, with the memories of St. Bartholomew's massacre still fresh in their minds. Deadlock was eventually broken by the French envoy's largesse, combined with the unconditional acceptance on Henri's behalf not only of the Warsaw Confederation on religious tolerance, but also of everything else the gentry had asked for. Thus another important precedent was established: from that time each successive King had to accept under oath a set of conditions confirming all the rights and privileges of the gentry and limiting his powers very severely. Should the King break this oath, his subjects would regard themselves as released from their oath of allegiance to the Crown. This became the basis of that other Polish institution—the legal rebellion justified by the real or alleged breach of his oath by a monarch.

A year and a half after Sigismund Augustus's death Henri arrived in Poland and was crowned in Cracow. But he found the restrictions imposed on him irksome and the opposition to his ham-fisted methods intolerable. With relief he learnt about the death of his brother and secretly fled from Poland to claim the French throne. His Polish reign had lasted exactly four months. The Poles did not realize how lucky they were to be rid of him; he became France's most incompetent King.

A second interregnum followed, even more disastrous. At first the Primate refused to declare the throne vacant and Henri was offered a chance to return, but he was in no hurry. Profiting from the chaos a powerful Tartar force raided the eastern provinces inflicting much damage and at last the Primate acted, setting the electoral machinery into motion. This time only some ten thousand gentry assembled near Warsaw to choose a new king.

The long delay—nearly a year and a half had elapsed since Henri's flight—gave foreign powers plenty of time to plot among themselves for the Polish succession and to influence leading Polish politicians by arguments and bribery. Emperor Maximillian II was particularly anxious to secure the Polish throne for himself or one of his sons; this would have ensured Austria's dominant position in Europe and made a decisive defeat of the Turks possible. In an attempt to gain the support of Ivan the Terrible, who once more was a candidate for the Polish crown, the Austrians proposed a partition of Turkey between Russia and the Empire, but Ivan was not tempted by so uncertain a prize. Instead he suggested a partition of Poland, with one of his sons taking over the Grand Duchy of Lithuania, while Poland proper would go to Austria. Maximillian, on his part, was so sure of winning the election—most of the bishops and senators were committed to vote for him—that he would not hear of carving up a state that was bound to be his.

The standing feud between Vienna and Paris meant that the French were interested in preventing the Hapsburgs from gaining the Polish crown and Henri III foolishly again offered himself for election. He stood no chance at all it seemed, nor did the Swedish, Italian, Bohemian and Transylvanian candidates.

When the election meetings started, the Senate voted overwhelmingly in favour of Maximillian. The gentry, always averse to Germans on the Polish throne, and after the experience with Henri prejudiced against all foreigners, gave an equally overwhelming majority in favour of a native candidate. They put forward two names, the Senate rejected them both. It looked as if the deadlock would have to be resolved by arms, but at the last moment a mixed commission was appointed to work out a compromise. The commission soon found its task impossible, but even before it concluded its deliberations the Papal Nuncio prevailed on the Primate to proclaim the election of Maximillian. The gentry, sword in hand, swore that they would never endorse this illegal act and would rather die than to see a Hapsburg on the throne. By a vast majority they proceeded to elect the Transylvanian prince, Stephen Batory, on condition that he married Anne Jagiellon, the sister of the late Sigismund Augustus.

Each side now offered the crown to its chosen candidate, and both accepted, Stephen Batory at once, Maximillian after some delay, while he negotiated for Russian support. By the time the Emperor said 'yes', a Diet attended by twenty thousand gentry declared his election null and void; Stephen Batory was already on his way to Cracow and was crowned there (29th April 1576). A short and localized civil war followed before Batory gained full control (Poland was less lucky during some subsequent elections) and four years after the death of the last in Jagiello's line the country had a proper king once more.

Stephen Batory turned out to be a good king with the will and ability to govern, and also a brilliant soldier, but his death after a reign of only ten years threw the country once more into the chaos of another election, another bout of international intrigue, corruption, the eventual split election and a threat of civil war. No lessons had been learnt from the first two interregna and there was worse to come—a complete paralysis of Parliament.

Poland's great pride, her parliamentary system, emerged gradually during the fifteenth and sixteenth centuries. Parliament consisted of the King, the Senate composed of *ex officio* members, and the Chamber of Deputies elected by the gentry on a constituency basis. The powers of this lower Chamber had grown steadily and from the beginning it was supposed to operate according to the rule of unanimity. After a debate on a proposed measure the Marshal (Speaker) of the Seym would ask if the Chamber was unanimous. Should any one member express dissent, the debate would be resumed and continue until such time as unanimity was achieved by persuasion, compromise or the intimidation of the minority. If no such agreement could be reached during the six weeks' session, the Seym was adjourned, normally for two years, without any decision having been recorded.

An attempt during the Jagiellonian period to substitute qualified majority for the rule of unanimity was defeated by the gentry. On the other hand the Deputies behaved with reasonable responsibility and during the sixteenth century there were only few occasions when the Seym failed to agree. They became much more frequent during the following hundred years, which saw the emergence of the *liberum veto*, by which the dissenting voice of one single Deputy could invalidate the whole proceedings of the Diet and break up the session.

The *veto* was first used in 1652 and, unbelievable as it may seem, it was hailed as a blessing by the Marshal of the Seym, Andrew Maximillian Fredro, because it prevented 'the stupid majority from ordering about the wise minority'.

Alas, the minority often lacked wisdom and not infrequently it was also corrupt. More and more often the Diets met to no purpose at all. Reform of the Constitution and any new legislation became almost impossible. The Polish Parliament became frozen by *the veto*. By that time also the idea of legal rebellion against the king, who had allegedly broken his coronation oath, had already been put into practice. The Poles had a word for it—*rokosz*—an armed confederation of the gentry against a real or imaginary royal threat to their liberties. And the gentry claimed to be the sole judge in each case.

Thus the three main tools of anarchy had been fully forged. But most Poles were not worried at all. They shared the views of Marshal Fredro, that 'Poland's strength lies in anarchy'.

7

WHITE EAGLES IN THE KREMLIN

For centuries Poland and Russia have been playing a gigantic tug of war over the plains of eastern Europe. The prize: domination of that part of the continent. Since there are no major natural obstacles between Warsaw and Moscow or between Cracow and Kiev, the actual frontier between the two countries has always been a function of their relative strength. In the end the Russians have won decisively, but there was a time when the boot was on the other foot, when flags with white Polish eagles were flying from the towers of the Kremlin, and the kings of Poland dreamt of a union of the two countries or even a conquest of all Russia.

Poland's territorial expansion in the fourteenth and fifteenth centuries, primarily due to her union with Lithuania, was phenomenal. When Casimir the Great came to the throne (1333) Poland was not much larger than present-day Portugal. When Casimir Jagiellon finally tamed the Teutonic Knights and regained Pomerania (1466) he ruled directly or indirectly over more than half a million square miles, an empire the size of France, Spain and Italy put together.

The major part of this empire was represented by the Grand Duchy of Lithuania which, profiting from the weakness of divided Russia, had extended south and east, reaching the Black Sea between the Crimea and the mouth of the River Dnieper. It included not only the whole of present-day Byelorussia, practically the whole of the Ukraine, but also parts of Russia proper.

Under the tolerant rule of the Jagiellon dynasty the diverse constituent parts of this empire started to grow together and coalesce. It looked as if the Polish super-state was there to stay. Even when the power of Moscow began to rise, when its dukes proclaimed themselves Tsars of all Russia and started to nibble at the Lithuanian conquests, even then it seemed that in terms of culture, civilization, wealth, power and the attractiveness of the political climate, the dice were heavily loaded in Poland's favour.

But just when they were at the summit, the Poles started to make those fatal mistakes which were to bring the downfall of their state. The crazy political system, which grew up in the sixteenth and degenerated in the seventeenth century, was enough to bring disaster, but the Polish gentry, as if driven by an instinct for self-destruction, also chose many kings who followed fatal foreign and domestic policies.

The first real trial of strength between Poland and Russia came during the reign of Stephen Batory who was elected in 1576 by the votes of the gentry, while the great nobles in the Senate had proclaimed Emperor Maximillion II as King of Poland.

Stephen Batory's first task had to be the suppression of pockets of resistance loyal to his rival. Profiting from Batory's preoccupations, Ivan the Terrible invaded the Polish part of the Baltic province of Livonia (Latvia).

Batory regarded this as a serious threat to Poland's northern flank, foreshadowing a Russian drive towards Lithuania and East Prussia. In a speech to the Seym, he convinced the deputies that Ivan's aim was the mastery of the Baltic. The Diet voted money for a war against Moscow. In two brilliant campaigns Batory defeated Ivan the Terrible and advanced deep into Russian territory, but he had to stop short of total victory because the Diet refused to vote further funds. With the mediation of the Holy See a truce was concluded, restoring Livonia and one other province to Poland, but leaving in Russian hands a large part of the territories taken from Lithuania earlier in the century. In conversation with the Papal Nuncio, Batory admitted that his ambition had been the conquest of Russia; he also made an unsuccessful attempt to link the two countries by personal union after Ivan's death.

The next major episode in Polish-Russian relations, and the unhappy climax to the phase of Polish domination, came just over twenty years later. It concerned Tsar Boris Godunov and the false Dimitri; Mussorgsky's well known opera has immortalized some aspects of this complicated and almost unbelievable series of events.

Poland had changed considerably in the intervening years. The shrewd Stephen Batory was succeeded by the ambitious Sigismund III (1587–1632), the first of the Vasa dynasty, who involved Poland in a series of disastrous wars for Swedish succession. Sigismund, a nephew of the last Jagiellonians, was a staunch Roman Catholic and having inherited the Swedish Crown five years after his election in Poland, he could not gain the support of his new Protestant subjects. However, neither he nor his successors ever gave up the claim to the Stockholm throne.

In Poland the icy wind of the counter-Reformation was now blowing hard. Batory had accepted the decisions of the Council of Trent and encouraged the Jesuits, but he would not allow any persecution of non-Catholics. Sigismund did not go out of his way to protect the dissidents. His closest friends and advisers were members of the Roman Catholic clergy, many of them Jesuits. In the words of a Polish historian[1] he was a 'zealous crusader for God, the Catholic Faith and the Vasa dynasty'. It was Sigismund who started the move to identify the monarchy and the whole country with the Church of Rome. He also fostered the Uniate movement, which brought the majority of the Orthodox bishops in Poland into communion with Rome, but which divided his Ruthenian subjects deeply and led to endless conflicts.

At this stage Boris Godunov and the false Dimitri appeared on the scene. Boris, the Tsar of Moscow, had been accused of murdering Dimitri, a son of Ivan the Terrible and the legitimate heir to the throne. Five years after Boris's coronation, a Russian adventurer, claiming to be Dimitri, arrived in Poland, accepted the Roman faith and married Marina Mniszek, an ambitious Polish woman of noble birth. Soon he started recruiting an army and prepared to fight for the Russian crown. Sigismund III watched these developments with interest, received the false Dimitri in audience and, though he gave him no official support, he placed no obstacles in his path.

Dimitri invaded Russia with an army of Polish and Cossack mercenaries, defeated Boris Godunov and, after the latter's sudden death, entered Moscow with his mercenaries and became Tsar, in June 1605. His Polish wife followed him several months

[1] Prof. F. Novak: *The Cambridge History of Poland*, Cambridge, 1950.

later and was crowned Tsarina (8th May 1606). Ten days later Dimitri was dead, murdered by Prince Vasili Shouiski, who in turn proclaimed himself Tsar and ordered a massacre of the Poles in Moscow.

That might have been the end of the episode but for the appearance of yet another false Dimitri. He, too, recruited an army in Poland and at the head of 18,000 mercenaries set out on a conquest of Moscow. Marina, the widow of the first false Dimitri, astonished the world by joining the second usurper and acknowledging him as her husband.

So far Sigismund had not taken any active part in the struggle for the Russian crown. When, however, Tsar Vasili, threatened by Dimitri's Polish mercenaries, concluded an alliance with Charles IX of Sweden, Sigismund intervened. 'Here was an opportunity for the King of Poland to identify his dynastic interests and his Catholic crusading zeal with the interests of the Polish nation.'[1] Without even consulting the Diet, Sigismund announced his own claim to the throne of the Tsars and invaded Russia. Tsar Vasili Shuiski proclaimed a holy war against what he regarded as a fanatical Catholic crusade by his imperialist neighbour.

At first the war went well for Sigismund. His Commander-in-Chief, the brilliant and wise Hetman Zolkiewski, inflicted a decisive defeat on the combined Russian-Swedish army. Shouiski was deposed and there was a chance of affecting a union between Poland and Moscow. Sigismund threw that chance away. He would not listen to Zolkiewski, who advocated a conciliatory approach. When Zolkiewski entered Moscow and, in accordance with an agreement that the King himself had signed with Russian representatives, persuaded the Boyars to offer the crown to Sigismund's son (Ladislas), the King suddenly changed his mind and demanded the Moscow throne for himself. The Russians, afraid of Sigismund's religious intolerance, would not hear of it, and rose in arms against the Poles. It was a cruel, religious war of national liberation. The Polish garrison had to withdraw into the Kremlin, withstood a siege lasting more than a year and a half, until hunger forced it to surrender.

By the end of 1612 Sigismund had to withdraw from Russia

[1] Novak, op. cit.

and abandon hope of gaining the crown of Moscow. His campaign had achieved the temporary return to Lithuania of Smolensk and Seversk, but the cost of this in terms of future Polish-Russian relations was incalculable.

His son, Ladislas IV, went to war twice laying claim to the crown he had lost because of his father. Each time he was repelled. Each time the Russians proclaimed a holy war against the Polish invaders. After that the kings of Poland had to give up their dreams of dominion over Russia, for now their country was quickly sliding towards disaster.

A state like Poland, where the peoples of different regions speak different tongues and worship in different churches, can survive only if its rulers pursue a consistent policy: it can either develop on federal, or at least semi-federal lines, which allow considerable freedom and autonomy to the constituent parts, relying on the economic, cultural and political advantages of size to hold the country together, or it can become a strongly centralized state, firmly imposing uniformity, and welding the whole into one nation. The Poles did neither.

Under Jagiellonian rule they started to pursue the first policy with a considerable measure of success. But under the elected kings they abandoned religious toleration, without substituting for it a ruthless drive to impose Roman Catholicism. In this way the Poles achieved a great deal of ill will without significant unifying results. At the same time, while there was some movement of Poles into the more sparsely populated eastern territories, this never took the form of systematic colonization on the lines the Germans had pursued so effectively in the west. Nor was there any serious attempt to impose the Polish language on the masses of the population in the eastern parts of the country. Only at the highest educational level did Polish culture exercise an overwhelming pull, especially after the establishment of two new universities (Vilno in 1578 and Lvov in 1661).

The result was the Polonization of the ruling class only, leaving the masses untouched. The gentry and the great nobles spoke Polish and regarded themselves as Poles, even if they were in origin Lithuanian, like the Radziwills, or Ukrainian, like the Wisniowieckis. This only aggravated the gulf between the peasants, who represented about ninety per cent of the population, and the gentry. Simultaneously the lot of the peasants deteriorated in a dramatic fashion. The size of their holdings decreased, they were not allowed to leave their villages and were required to work a certain number of days on the squire's land. At the beginning of the sixteenth century this servitude amounted to one or two days per week, but in the seventeenth century six days a week became not uncommon. Since disputes between the peasants and their squires had been removed from Royal jurisdiction early in the sixteenth century, the peasant was not only a serf, but a defenceless serf at that.

The condition of the peasant had become so pitiful by the end of the sixteenth century that the eloquent Jesuit preacher, Peter Skarga, in a series of sermons to the Diet (1597) protested against the system in no uncertain terms.

> . . . laws without Equity, laws twisted by human injustice, are not laws but evil itself, for Justice must be the foundation of every Commonwealth. . . .
>
> Let me mention the bad law which turns peasants, free men, Poles and faithful Christians, into poor, subject slaves, as if they had been bought in the market place or captured in a just war; and others do with them what they like, allowing them no defence of their property, person or life, giving them no Court in which they could seek redress for the often intolerable wrongs, exercising over them the very *supremum dominium* from which we all recoil.

The gentry remained deaf to Skarga's pleadings and for the peasants matters went from bad to worse. Two hundred years later Hugo Kollontaj, one of the leaders of the long overdue movement for reform, wrote in 1791 that comparisons of Poland with Turkey were not altogether unfair: 'The only difference is that there the same despot gives orders to the Moslem and the Greek alike, while here a hundred thousand noble families form an aristocratic-feudal nation, keeping the remaining millions of people as foreign slaves.'

Another reformer, Stanislas Staszic wrote (1790):

> I can see millions of people, some half naked, some dressed in skins or rough cloth, all emaciated, wasted, reduced to misery. . . . Sullen, stunned and stupid, they feel little and think little: this is their greatest happiness. . . . This, my good compatriots, is the joyous condition of the people on whom the fate of the Commonwealth depends! These are the men who are feeding you. This is the fate of the peasant in Poland!

Reduced to this condition, half-starved and illiterate, the peasants showed no national consciousness, but they were divided by language and religion. On the whole the Roman Catholics spoke Polish or Lithuanian, the Greek Orthodox or Uniate spoke White Russian (Byelorussian) or Ruthenian (Ukrainian). Occasionally the peasants tried to revolt against their masters, but they never succeeded, except in the Ukraine where the Cossacks achieved a remarkable degree of freedom. And there a selfish and shortsighted policy pushed them into the arms of Moscow.

The Cossacks owed their name to the Turks and their existence to the Tartars. The word 'Cossack' means a homeless, independent adventurer. It was given towards the end of the fifteenth century to the members of a strange community, which grew up in a part of the Ukraine as the result of constant predatory raids by the Tartars from the Crimea. Some 150 miles south-east from the ancient city of Kiev began a vast no-man's-land so frequently raided by the Tartars that villages had disappeared and the cultivation of the soil had to be abandoned. This huge stretch of the Ukranian steppe (some 30,000 square miles) was given the name of the Wild Plains—the prototype of the American Wild West.

In the Wild Plains there was no gentry, no landlords, no established authority and no law. Life was dangerous because of the frequent and savage Tartar raids, but it was completely free. This attracted courageous and restless spirits from the Ukraine and farther afield, including many peasants who had found life in villages intolerable. Fully armed, and organized in troops for protection against the Tartars, they made a living by hunting, fishing and rounding up the cattle which roamed the steppes.

Gradually the Cossacks became so strong and numerous that they could challenge the Tartars and even make effective raids into the Crimea. Their success in breaking the terror of the Tartars enabled the landlords to drift back into that part of the Ukraine, and they in turn attracted settlers from the west by promises of at least temporary immunity from taxes and all the burdens of serfdom. The pioneer Cossacks resisted this intrusion of the gentry and, encouraged by their example, the new settlers revolted as soon as the nobles tried to extract from them what they regarded as their due.

By the middle of the sixteenth century the Cossacks were sufficiently well organized to conduct their own policy. When the Polish authorities viewed this with disfavour, they turned for a time to Ivan the Terrible, but soon returned to a fiercely independent line. Polish kings started recruiting Cossacks into special cavalry detachments of their army—they made excellent soldiers—granting them immunity from the jurisdiction of the civil authorities. Though the numbers concerned were small, the idea spread among the Cossacks that they should all be regarded as soldiers and be free from serfdom. In the eyes of the landlords this was rebellion which had to be suppressed and the system of servitude restored. Since the land-owning class was in the main Polish, or at least Polish speaking and largely Catholic, and the Cossacks were predominantly Ukranian and Greek Orthodox, the situation became explosive.

It erupted for the first time in 1595 in a Cossack revolt, which started as a rising against a local prince, but turned the following year into a successful religious war in defence of the Greek Orthodox against the Uniate Church. In the end a Polish army crushed the Cossacks, but soon they regained their former strength and once more became a military force to be reckoned with. In 1621 their army, 40,000 strong, helped the Poles defeat a Turkish invasion.

But the Polish gentry, especially the great landowners and the Roman Catholic clergy, were still unwilling to grant even the minimum Cossack demands, which amounted to freedom from servitude and freedom for the Greek Orthodox Church. For over thirty years Cossack revolts, followed by never totally effective Polish punitive expeditions, helped to sap the strength of the Polish-Lithuanian Commonwealth. At last, the Cossack leader, Bohdan Chmielnicki, sought the protection of Moscow. In a solemn treaty (18th January 1654) the Tsar guaranteed all the Cossack rights and privileges. Chmielnicki was not to know that this guarantee was not worth the parchment on which it was written. The Cossacks had simply exchanged one yoke for another, a more ruthless and efficient one. The Poles lost the eastern Ukraine, including the city of Kiev, and prepared the ground for a further Russian advance to the west.

8

THE FALL OF THE COMMONWEALTH

It is impossible to decide when the Polish Commonwealth reached the lowest point of its fortunes. The middle of the seventeenth century saw a series of devastating wars with the Cossacks, Russians, Turks and Swedes. Aided and abetted by ambitious magnates, foreign armies marched across Poland, leaving a wasteland behind them. At one stage practically the whole country was in Swedish hands and King John Casimir, the last of the Vasa dynasty, had to flee across the border into Silesia. It looked like the end of Poland.

Then came one of those surprising turns of fortune which abound in the history of Poland. Since the Swedes were treating Poland as a conquered territory, robbing churches and castles, pillaging towns and terrorizing the population, the unavoidable reaction set in. Pockets of resistance began to appear in various parts of the country. The monastery which houses the famous picture of the Black Madonna, at Czestochowa, was one of them. It successfully resisted a forty-day siege by a Swedish army. When, on the day following Christmas 1655, the Swedes withdrew, this was hailed as a miracle and became the turning point of the war.

Suddenly the nation rallied around the King, who promptly returned from exile. On entering the city of Lvov, John Casimir took a double vow in public: henceforth the Blessed Virgin Mary was to be venerated as 'the Queen of Poland' and, in recognition of the help he had received from the peasants, the King promised that after the end of the war he would try to free the people of the Kingdom 'from all the burdens and wrongs of oppression'. The first vow proved much easier to keep than the second. A wave of religious fanaticism swept Poland and in its wake came the persecution of Protestants and Jews, culminating in the total banishment from the country of all members of the most radical of all the Protestant sects, known as Arians

(Polish Brethren or Anti-Trinitarians), who preached complete religious freedom and social reforms far in advance of their time. But the lasting effect of the defence of Czestochowa and of John Casimir's vow has been the identification of the Polish nation with the Roman Catholic faith and the cult of the Virgin Mary, which flourishes to this day, attracting each year hundreds of thousands of pilgrims to the shrine of the Black Madonna.

Nothing much came of John Casimir's second vow, which was taken to imply a promise to abolish the servitude of the peasants. He did free a small number of them, those who had distinguished themselves in the war, but he was unable to do anything for the masses. In the end, having fought more disastrous wars, having lost East Prussia and eastern Ukraine, and having failed to reform the Constitution, the embittered John Casimir gave up the throne (1668) and retired to France. In his abdication address he warned the nation that the Kingdom could not survive under the existing system.

Indeed, already during his reign, the first agreement on the partition of Poland had been drawn up. A treaty signed at Radnot in Hungary (1656) divided Poland between Sweden, Brandenburg (Prussia), Transylvania and the Cossacks, with one of the Radziwill family obtaining a large province as an independent duchy. But this did not suit either Russia or the Hapsburg Empire. Poland was given a century of grace.

The country seemed beyond salvation. Utterly devastated by wars, diminished in size, torn by internal dissention and foreign intrigue, paralysed by the *liberum veto* and frequent rebellions, Poland was a temptation to her neighbours. The first to pounce was Turkey. Armies of the Sultan marched into what was left of Polish Ukraine and imposed a humiliating treaty. Poland not only lost three provinces, but had to undertake to pay tribute to the Sultan.

The news of this treaty made Polish blood boil. For once united, the Diet of 1673 promptly voted enough money to raise an army of fifty thousand. Under the brilliant command of John Sobieski this army defeated the Turks and restored the *status quo*. Hailed as a hero, Sobieski was elected to the throne, which had just fallen vacant. Ten years later he led another Polish army on the famous expedition to the rescue of Vienna, the decisive defeat of the Ottoman Empire, and the last great victory to be won by the doomed Kingdom.

There was little in the next hundred years of Polish history to make even the most fervent patriot proud of his nation. Poland was in decay—moral, cultural, economic and political decay. Two disastrously long reigns by German kings from Saxony, Augustus II and Augustus III, both imposed on Poland by her neighbours who used bribery and intimidation, turned the country into a pawn of the great powers.

At that very time the cruel rhythm of history gave both Russia and Prussia outstanding and unscrupulous leaders in Peter the Great, Catherine II and Frederick the Great. It was their century, the period of aggressive power in central and eastern Europe, directed from St. Petersburg and from Berlin. With Poland representing a power vacuum, her fate was sealed, and it might seem surprising she survived so long. In fact the Prussians had been pressing for a partition already at the beginning of the eighteenth century, but the Russians would not agree because Peter the Great had a more ambitious objective in mind—the annexation of the whole country.

Indeed Russia soon became the true master of Poland. Her army was decisive in placing Augustus III on the throne in opposition to the majority of electors, who wanted Stanislas Leszczynski as King. And the supreme irony: the absolute rulers of Russia and Prussia now became the joint guarantors and the most active champions of Polish constitutional liberties. The perpetuation of the anarchy engendered by the *liberum veto* and the legalized rebellions was very much in their interest.

The last Polish king, Stanislas Poniatowski (1764–95), owed his nomination to a whim of Catherine II and his election to another armed intervention by Russia. This well educated, handsome Polish noble, three years younger than Catherine, had been one of her lovers while on a diplomatic mission to St. Petersburg. Through the bed of the Empress of Russia to the Polish throne—that was the measure of the downfall of the once proud and powerful Commonwealth.

But already during the reign of Augustus III enlightened voices could be heard, demanding a drastic reform of the constitution and of the social system. Under Stanislas Augustus these voices became a loud and influential chorus. *Monitor*, a periodical modelled on the London *Spectator*, started publication in 1765 and soon became the main forum for reformist views. It lashed out against the conservatism and obscurantism of the gentry, advocated religious tolerance, the extension of the franchise, improvements in the lot of the peasant and changes in the constitution.

The reformists, who grew in numbers and enjoyed the sympathy of the King, were however far from united. Worse still, on only one point, that of religious tolerance, could they count on the support of Russia and Prussia, whose protectorate Poland then was in fact, if not in name. Russia naturally wanted equal rights for the Greek Orthodox, Prussia for the Protestants. But neither would hear of a reform of the Constitution, and especially the abolition of the *liberum veto*. In the words of Frederick the Great, it was important 'to keep Poland in a coma'.

But the Poles were no longer comatose. In 1768 a confederation formed in the town of Bar gave the signal for an uprising of the gentry against the King and the Russian domination of the country. The fighting lasted four years, a civil war in fact, but with the Russian army playing the decisive part. When the confederates were crushed the Russians deported 5,000 of them to Siberia, but many managed to escape abroad. Among them was Casimir Pulaski, who went to America, took part in the United States' war of independence and was killed in the Battle of Savannah.

The unsuccessful confederation gave Poland's neighbours an excuse for the first partition of the country. They claimed, not without justification, that 'the spirit of faction in Poland led to anarchy' and, with less veracity, that there was 'a total disintegration of the State'. By a series of treaties signed in St. Petersburg on 5th August 1772, Russia, Austria and Prussia annexed between them some 84,000 square miles (an area larger than England and Wales) with a population of four and a half million. The Polish Diet, partly bribed and partly browbeaten by threats of further annexations, ratified the partition.

The shock of these events at last stimulated the overdue reforms. Sensibly enough the first major changes were in the field of education. Poland used to have a good educational

The Kings of the Jagiellonian dynasty transformed Wawel Castle into a magnificent Renaissance palace. Tournaments were held in the central courtyard (*above*). Priceless Gobelin tapestries adorned the walls of the State rooms (*below*)

Adam Mickiewicz (1798–1855), Poland's greatest poet and one of the leaders of the romantic emigration in France

Frederic Chopin (1810–1849), also an exile, expressed in music the anguish of a nation struggling for survival

system with a school in every parish and three universities, but this had declined and degenerated to an unbelievable degree. Even a large proportion of the gentry was illiterate and those who did go to school received instruction that was not only

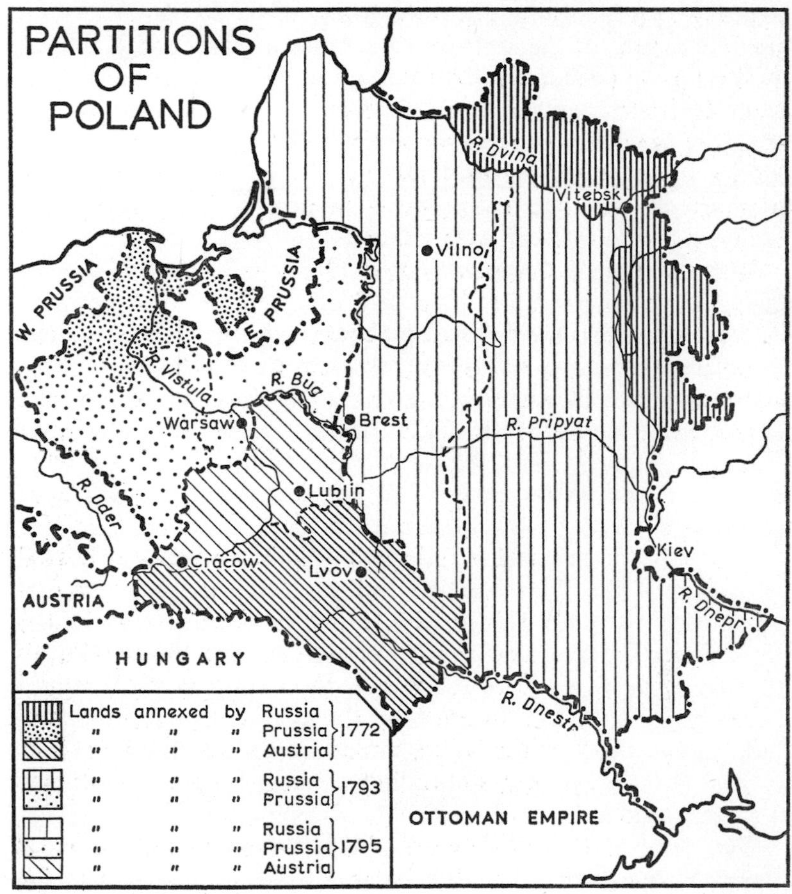

utterly out-of-date, but completely irrelevant to the needs of the day.

The dissolution of the Jesuit Order by the Pope in 1773 gave the reformers a chance to make a fresh start. The Jesuits had in Poland more than fifty colleges with some 20,000 pupils and also considerable estates. All this property was turned over to a new body, the Commission for National Education, which immediately set about giving the country a modern school system as an essential foundation for further reform.

At the same time a tidal wave of political pamphleteering hit the literate public, stimulating a ferment of ideas even greater and more profound than in the hey-day of the Reformation. As the last decade of the eighteenth century approached it looked as if not only France but also Poland was heading for a revolution. In both countries the reformers were influenced by the ideas of Jean-Jaques Rousseau. In both the existing state of affairs was regarded as intolerable and the demand for change increasingly insistent, culminating in new constitutions voted within a few months of each other.

But the Polish Constitution of 3rd May 1791 is a very different document from the one adopted by the National Assembly in Paris the following September, for in the event the Poles did not have a revolution, though the changes they introduced were revolutionary in their peculiar circumstances. While the French were storming the Bastille under the slogan of 'Liberty, Equality and Fraternity', enlightened Poles were struggling against an excess of liberty and the weakness of authority.

The Polish Constitution, adopted after three years of heated argument in the Diet, and passed while the majority of die-hards was away on Easter holiday, took several steps in the right direction. It abolished the *liberum veto* and the election of the King, substituting for them majority voting in the Diet and hereditary monarchy; it separated the legislative, executive and judicial functions of the State, introduced a sensible system of central government and a standing army; it turned Poland into a modern state.

The Poles were justly proud of this Constitution. It was all the more remarkable because its authors were members of the gentry, who were surrendering some of their most cherished privileges. They even extended the franchise to the burghers and allowed them to hold offices of State. In one direction only they shrank from taking the decisive step, even if many of them wanted to: they left the peasants in servitude. True, the peasant was given once more the protection of the law, but he remained a serf Paradoxically, he could gain his freedom only by first escaping abroad and then returning to Poland, for the Constitution proclaimed:

'We declare . . . that any man entering the Commonwealth or returning to it from any direction, from the moment he sets foot on Polish soil becomes free to exercise his industry wherever and however he wants.'

In retrospect it is easy to argue that as long as nearly 90 per cent of the population remained in servitude and utter poverty, Poland had no chance of mobilizing and releasing the energies of the whole nation. For the majority of Polish Deputies in 1791 the nation still consisted of the gentry and, somewhat grudgingly, the middle classes (a similar system prevailed in all the neighbouring countries). But to reproach the Poles for not freeing the peasants at that time would be as reasonable as to blame the authors of the United States Constitution for not freeing the slaves in 1787.

Even if the Polish reformers did not achieve freedom and equality for the majority, they gave the country a Constitution which eliminated most of past weakness and introduced a system under which Poland had a chance of survival. Her neighbours saw to it that the attempt was abortive. The rulers of Russia and Prussia detected in the Constitution another symptom of the 'French plague' and regarded its moderate authors as a lot of Polish Jacobins. Using a group of dissatisfied Polish nobles to start a rebellion against the Constitution, Catherine sent the Russian army to their aid. After three months of stubborn fighting the reactionaries and their Russian allies won and a new Polish Diet was forced to annul the Constitution. Even that was not enough to satisfy the Russians and the Prussians. A second partition of Poland followed in 1793 with Russia annexing about 100,000 square miles in the east, Prussia only just over 20,000 square miles in the north-west, including the rich prize of the city of Gdansk. (Austria did not take part that time.)

After the second partition Poland was still about the size of Great Britain, but it was a disorganized rump of a state, independent only in name, forced to keep an army of occupation 40,000 strong. It was a hopeless and humiliating situation, which the Poles were not prepared to accept, even if their Diet was again browbeaten into ratifying the partition.

On 24th March 1794, in the great square in Cracow, General Thaddeus Kosciuszko, already a hero of the American War of Independence, and of the recent fighting against the Russians, proclaimed a national insurrection. The odds against him looked hopeless, yet he nearly succeeded. One of his first acts granted the peasants the right to leave their villages, reduced the amount of servitude and gave special privileges to those who took up arms under his command. The response was enthusiastic and soon the whole of Poland was ablaze. Kosciuszko's skilful tactics freed Warsaw and defeated the Russians in several battles. At the same time he was careful not to provoke the Prussians, hoping in vain that they would remain neutral. When the Prussians did intervene, and together with the Russians lay siege to Warsaw, the situation looked hopeless. Still the city defended itself and the fight went on until Kosciuszko himself, wounded in battle, was taken prisoner by the Russians. Only then did the Russians take Warsaw by storm and the Insurrection collapsed (5th November 1794) to be followed quickly by the third and last partition of Poland. In 1795 Russia, Austria and Prussia divided between themselves what was left of the Polish State. The Prussian share was the most valuable and included Warsaw itself.

And so Poland disappeared from the map of Europe. But Kosciuszko's insurrection, though it failed to save the State, had a profound effect on the nation. Under his flag, for the first time in history, the various social and religious groups came together; nobles and peasants, town and country, Catholics and Protestants, Greek Orthodox and Jews fought side by side. They lost, but their fight helped to strengthen national consciousness.

Kosciuszko himself, now an almost legendary figure, released by the Russians, went into exile. In his will he left all his property in the United States to his friend, Thomas Jefferson, with the express wish that it should be used to buy the freedom of negro slaves. After his death the Americans named after him a County in the State of Indiana and a town in Mississippi. The Poles transported his body to Cracow and buried it in the Wawel Cathedral next to Kings John Sobieski and Stephen Batory. They also paid him a unique honour of building outside Cracow a huge memorial mound which bears his name.

PART THREE

UNDER PARTITIONS

9

INQUEST AND REBURIAL

When a state dies and disappears from the map, as Poland did in 1795, an inquest is inevitable. The Poles have been holding one ever since and they are still not agreed on the verdict—they probably never will be. To an outsider the discussion may seem largely academic, but during the 120 years of Poland's partitions, during the desperate search for national rebirth and the fight for independence, for the Poles it had an all-important and painful relevance. Even today the controversy about the causes of the disaster in the eighteenth century is not quite divorced from the political realities of Po and.

Why then did the Polish state perish in 1795? Some of the causes are obvious: anarchy and internal weakness, which coincided with an expansionist period among Poland's neighbours. But was that all? Was there perhaps a metaphysical reason? 'Poland is the Christ of nations,' proclaimed her romantic poets in the nineteenth century, 'destined to suffer in her messianic role for the sake of the redemption of all nations.'

Some Poles blamed only themselves and their leaders. In the heat of an insurrection against the Russians in 1830 one of its moving spirits, Maurice Mochnacki, published under the title *To be or not to be*, this analysis of the problem:

> A great nation in the centre of Europe fell by the impotence of the Constitution, it fell by the many faults of its structure. We did not perish because we had traitors in our midst, because we quarrelled, because Moscow had trouble maker in its pay. . . . These were only the results of a far more deep-rooted evil. We perished because not the majority but the minority has been the nation. We perished because no social revolution had changed this ill relationship. The evil was basic; Kosciuszko raised his sword in the cause of an insurrection, but he should have fought in the cause of social revolution. . . . Kosciuszko was a decent Pole, he was brave knight; but his

reasoning was false. To save the country it was necessary to destroy the internal evil; he preferred to succumb to an external foe. Poland needed an internal revolution; he turned the struggle outwards. Kosciuszko brought the doom of Poland.

There is much truth in this analysis and, not surprisingly, marxist historians see the oppression of the peasants as the chief cause of Poland's downfall. But they are kinder to Kosciuszko, who is allowed to remain a national hero. According to them it was largely sabotage on the part of the gentry that prevented Kosciuszko from mobilizing the whole nation.

On the other hand the leading *émigré* Polish historian, Professor O. Halecki, sees the picture in quite a different light:

> The Poles of the eighteenth century could not remedy this situation, because they had no longer the deep religious faith which had animated their ancestors when they tried the great experiement of the Royal Republic and defended the frontiers of Christendom. Hence, Providence sent them a great ordeal which was to purify the national soul and give their sons to behold in the humiliation of expiation a new historic mission, worthy of a great past.[1]

Thus the Poles agree on one point only—the roots of their country's disaster were mainly internal. Internal reform, however, was no longer in their power after the third partition—they were at the mercy of three absolute monarchs, who ruled them from Berlin, Vienna and St. Petersburg. There was little the Poles could achieve without outside help and immediately their eyes were attracted by revolutionary France, the chief enemy of absolute rulers.

Polish politicians and officers of Kosciuszko's disbanded army gravitated towards France. One of them, General John Henry Dombrowski, soon started negotiating for the formation of a Polish army in the west. His chance came when the French captured 30,000 Austrian soldiers in northern Italy, among them some 7,000 Polish conscripts. Having obtained Bonaparte's agreement, Dombrowski organized the Polish Legions in Lombardy (1797). The motto on their standards read: 'For your Freedom and ours!' Their song, the Dombrowski mazurka, was destined to become Poland's national anthem: 'Poland is not yet lost as long as we are alive.'

[1] *A History of Poland*, Dent, London, 1961.

'From the Italian soil to Poland . . .' sang the soldiers of the Legions as they marched into battle. But the road from Milan to Warsaw turned out to be not only long but also exceedingly winding. It took them first fighting into Rome and Naples, then to Germany and to San Domingo, where they were sent to suppress a Negro rising and died in their thousands from yellow fever. Of the twenty thousand soldiers who joined the Legions only about a quarter ever reached the Duchy of Warsaw, which Napoleon created in 1805 out of a part of the German share of Poland. This small, semi-autonomous state, later enlarged by the inclusion of some provinces taken from the Austrians, became the focus of Polish hopes.

Not all the Poles trusted the Emperor. Many of the great nobles regarded him as a dangerous revolutionary and they advocated co-operation with Russia. Others, like the revered leader of the insurrection of 1794, Thaddeus Kosciuszko, realized that Napoleon was only using Poland as a tool in his design of conquest. But the majority thought that collaboration with Napoleon would bring the rebirth of their country. They fought for him on all the battlefields of Europe, and, when the Grand Army set out on its ill-fated march on Moscow it included large Polish contingents. Nearly half of them were organized into an independent corps under Prince Joseph Poniatowski, a nephew of the last King of Poland.

The Poles were the first to storm their way into Smolensk, they led the attack at Borodino, they fought gallant rearguard actions during the terrible winter retreat from Moscow. A hundred thousand Poles took part in the Russian campaign; only thirty thousand came back. But those remained loyal to the end. Poniatowski himself, now a Marshal of France, was killed while covering Napoleon's retreat from Leipzig.

The dream of turning the Duchy of Warsaw into a nucleus of independent Poland turned out to be short-lived. Six years after Napoleon had created it, the Duchy was occupied by a vast Russian army, the country was in ruins, and countless Polish graves marked the path of the advances and retreats of the deposed French Emperor. Apart from heroic glory, the Poles gained little from linking their fate with Napoleon: his Civil Code was introduced into the Duchy of Warsaw (it remained in force until 1945) and the Polish question appeared in the agenda of the Congress of Vienna (1814–15), though Poland was not invited to send a representative.

The statesmen assembled in Vienna found the Polish question so intractable that at one stage they nearly went to war over it. Of the five major powers represented at Vienna, two—England and France—had no direct interest in Poland, but they were anxious to see that the Continent should be free from domination by a single country. Two others—Austria and Prussia—were anxious to recover their shares of the partitions of Poland. The third and the strongest—Russia—had far-reaching ambitions. All the five powers were united, however, in their anxiety to extinguish once and for all the embers of the French Revolution and to ensure the return of the old order to Europe. The Poles, having already gained for themselves the reputation of rebels and having fought under the colours of the revolution, were viewed with suspicion. When Castlereagh put forward a tentative proposal for the restoration of the Polish Kingdom within its pre-partition frontiers, the other envoys assumed, not entirely without reason, that this was just a tactical manœuvre and refused to consider it seriously.

Tsar Alexander I wanted to reunite the whole of Poland under his crown. This ambition fitted in with the ideas of some influential Poles in his entourage, led by Prince Adam Czartoryski, who had the confidence of the liberal-minded Tsar. But the vested interests of Prussia and Austria proved too strong, and Russia, though she was the most powerful European country, had to compromise. Alexander achieved his ambition of becoming King of Poland, a constitutional state linked by the Crown to absolutist Russia, but this new Kingdom, with Warsaw as its capital, was a pale shadow of its old self. Prussia and Austria surrendered only parts of their Polish conquests, while Russia kept all she had taken in the partitions. Cut off from the sea, with a territory of only 50,000 square miles and a population of 3,300,000, the Congress Kingdom, as it was called, was hardly a viable state. Inevitably it had to become a Russian colony.

It is worth noting that, with small changes only, the present Polish Soviet frontier drawn up by Stalin follows the line of the frontier between the Congress Kingdom and Tsarist Russia. But unlike Stalin, Alexander I, in an attempt to gain the co-operation of the Poles, dangled before them the prospect of reuniting the Congress Kingdom with the eastern lands formerly of the Polish-Lithuanian Commonwealth.

Another creation of the Congress of Vienna was the Free City of Cracow, a miniature Polish state of some 350 square miles with a population of under 100,000, which was put under 'the protection of Russia, Austria and Prussia'. It survived only until 1846 when it was incorporated into the Austrian Empire.

In all other respects the artificial frontiers drawn across Poland by the Congress of Vienna proved durable indeed. They lasted for a whole century and the Polish question did not surface as a live issue at any international conference until the Allied statesmen assembled in Paris in 1919. During the intervening hundred unhappy years the Poles, groaning under the yoke of Russia, Austria and Prussia, re-thinking their policies, taking to arms desperately at every opportunity, transformed themselves into a modern nation.

10

ROMANTIC GLORY

Until quite recently most Poles looked at the nineteenth century through romantic spectacles. Many still do. They can see in their mind's eye a series of vast, heroic canvasses depicting the key episodes in their ancestors' gallant but vain struggle to restore Poland to the ranks of independent nations:

1797	Polish Legions formed in Italy
1806	Napoleon's army enters Poland
1807	Creation of the Duchy of Warsaw
1809	War with Austria. Duchy of Warsaw enlarged
1812	100,000 Polish soldiers in Napoleon's march on Moscow
1813	Prince Poniatowski killed at Leipzig
1830–31	The November rising against the Russians
1846	Rising against the Austrians
1848	Rising against the Prussians
1848–49	Polish participation in the revolutionary movements in France, Italy, Germany, Austria, Hungary and Rumania
1863–64	The January rising against the Russians

Each rising, each revolution, was followed by more severe repression, by hangings and deportations, yet the flame of resistance continued to glow. This was indeed the heroic period of Polish history. But there were some Poles, few at first, who thought that all this heroic sacrifice was useless and that the future of the country lay in collaboration with Russia. The first leader of this movement was Prince Adam Czartoryski, a personal friend of Tsar Alexander I and an influential member of the councils of St. Petersburg.

Czartoryski was at Alexander's side during the Congress of Vienna and the Tsar tended to follow his advice rather than that of his Russian ministers. The resulting Congress Kingdom of

Poland was an anomaly in terms of ethnography, geography, economy and above all, politics. The absolute ruler of St. Petersburg sat on the Warsaw throne as a constitutional monarch and the Poles enjoyed a relatively liberal government, which was denied to the Russians. Castlereagh prophetically warned the Tsar the system could not last and would probably 'either be deliberately destroyed or perish at the hands of his successor'.

The majority of the Poles were of course dissatisfied with their small, landlocked, artificial kingdom, with the Tsar as their King, and with being a satellite of Russia. The Russian establishment, always anti-liberal, hated it for quite different reasons. Alexander himself adopted an equivocal attitude. In private he talked to the Poles about reuniting the Kingdom with Lithuania, which had been incorporated into Russia, in public he hinted at his desire to extend the liberal Polish constitution to all his lands, but at heart he remained an autocrat who resented any sign of opposition. Soon it became clear that he would abide by the constitution only in so far as it suited him.

Czartoryski, the experienced statesman, appeared to be the obvious choice for the important post of Alexander's viceroy in Warsaw but, perhaps fearing the Prince's independent mind, the Tsar sent him to Vilno as Chancellor of the University. A Polish general with a distinguished military record, but a complete political nonentity, was made viceroy. Under him a Russian-appointed Administrative Council performed the functions of a government; the real power remained in the hands of two Russians: The Tsar's High Commissioner, Count Novosiltsov, and the Commander-in-Chief of the Kingdom's army, Alexander's brother, the Grand Duke Constantine.

If Alexander was a civilized autocrat, his brother was an uncouth despot. He soon gained for himself the general hatred of the Poles, especially of the army, which he loved and terrorized at the same time. Yet, Grand Duke Constantine was not only married to a Polish woman, but had genuine sympathy for Polish national aspirations. At his express wish Alexander I had appointed him to command not only the army of the Congress Kingdom, but also the military units in Lithuania and other provinces incorporated into Russia, thus hinting at another promise of reunification. Nobody could have been more surprised than Constantine when his palace became the first target of Polish insurgents in November 1830 and he had to flee for his life.

In spite of mounting political tension, the peaceful and relatively stable years of 1815–30 brought considerable advantages to the Congress Kingdom. The ravages of Napoleonic wars were repaired, communications improved, industry developed, the Treasury reformed. . . . In 1817 the University of Warsaw was founded as the apex of an expanding system of education. In the provinces incorporated into Russia conditions were also on the whole tolerable and the ancient University of Vilno (founded by Stephen Batory in 1578) entered its most flourishing phase, becoming a very important centre of Polish learning and culture.

But the Poles were not a nation to settle down to a dull, peaceful and relatively prosperous existence under an alien rule. The whole of Europe was seething with romantic, revolutionary ideas and it would have been unnatural if the Poles had kept aloof. Secret organizations, some of them under the influence of the Italian Carbonari, some linked with the western Freemasons, all of them subscribing to democratic and patriotic aims, were springing up like mushrooms. They appealed especially to the students of the Universities of Warsaw and Vilno, young army officers, the growing ranks of the professional classes and the politically conscious gentry. This was the beginning of the Polish tradition of conspiracy against alien rule, a tradition which has flourished ever since.

The Russians were quick to recognize the danger. Their suspicious police pounced with severity against all secret organizations, however innocuous their aim might be, and their members risked at least deportation or several years in a Tsarist prison. When, after the death of Alexander I (1825), Nicholas I succeeded to the Russian and Polish thrones, the police discovered links between the Decabrist plot in Russia and Polish secret organizations. The regime became even more oppressive and by the summer of 1830 the situation in Warsaw became explosive. The news of the July revolution against the Bourbons in France, of the August Belgian rising against the Dutch and of riots in Germany had an electrifying impact on the population. The Russians realized that they were sitting on a powder keg, but knew not who would light the fuse, or where or when.

In fact it was the Tsar himself who lit it by planning to send Polish and Russian troops to suppress the revolutions in the west. When Warsaw newspapers on 19th and 20th November carried the first announcements of a mobilization, the conspirators knew that they had to strike. The military, who were prominent in the conspiracy, had no desire to help the Tsar in fighting the Belgians or their former French allies. Also the police had uncovered yet another secret student organization connected with the plot and the whole conspiracy was suddenly in danger.

It was, however, not a conspiracy on a national scale, it had no clear plan of action or even agreed long-term objectives. Little or no co-ordination had taken place between the various secret organizations and there was no recognized leadership—just a handful of young politicians and army officers determined to fight for Poland's independence. The plot itself was ill-prepared and nearly ended in immediate failure.

A fire in an old Warsaw brewery was to have been the signal for a general rising in the capital in the evening of 29th November. But the fire was started too early and was so small that it went unnoticed. Instead of a general rising only one group of conspirators and the students of the military academy went into action, attacking the residence of the Grand Duke Constantine. The Grand Duke managed to escape and the insurgents were nearly captured by the Russians. Such was the inauspicious beginning of the November rising, which was to stir the imagination of successive generations of Poles. Of all insurrections of the nineteenth century it had the greatest chance of success for the simple reason that thanks to Constantine an efficient Polish army existed, even though it numbered only some 40,000 men. But to succeed it needed good, single-minded political leaders and brilliant military commanders, capable of defeating far superior Russian forces. It had neither.

The insurgents themselves had no leaders who could command general support, and they allowed the Russian-appointed Administrative Council to continue in office. This was gradually enlarged and strengthened by the inclusion first of moderate conservatives, like Prince Adam Czartoryski, and later also radicals, like the young popular tribune Mochnacki and the distinguished historian, Lelewel. Like most coalitions, the Administrative Council, transformed into a Provisional Government, was split on all major issues of internal and foreign policy. The conservatives wished to negotiate with the Tsar, the radicals to depose him. Nicholas I forced the issue by refusing to parley with the Poles and by sending a large army to suppress the rising.

The first Polish Commander-in-Chief wasted precious weeks before he started building up the army; he did not believe in the possibility of victory. Yet, the Polish army grew and the rising spread to Lithuania, gaining some support from the peasants, even though the Diet failed to pass a law granting them land from the Royal estates. At first the Poles were successful in halting the onslaught of vastly superior Russian forces. But in the end the numerical superiority of the enemy, combined with grave mistakes made by a series of incompetent Polish Commanders-in-Chief—there were six of them in the course of ten months—produced the inevitable result. By September 1831 the Russians had fought their way into Warsaw, within a few weeks most Polish units had crossed into Austria and Prussia to be disarmed, and soon it was all over, except for the vengeance of the Tsar.

The French Foreign Minister, General Sebastiani, was able to reassure his compatriots, who had watched the struggle with sympathy and anxiety, that order had been restored in Warsaw. It was order achieved by deportations, prison and gallows. A savage wave of repression removed all vestiges of national autonomy. The Constitution of the Congress Kingdom was abolished, the Army dissolved, the University of Warsaw closed, historical treasures were removed to St. Petersburg and Russian became the official language. In everything but name the Congress Kingdom became a Russian colony. The Polish-Lithuanian provinces incorporated into Russia fared even worse, while the Austrians and Prussians also tightened the screws of oppression in their parts of the dismembered country.

Everywhere the Poles paid dearly for their eleven months of romantic glory. Now only in exile, in the West, could they speak their minds freely, give vent to their feelings and to plot for the liberation of Poland. From abroad they helped to organize resistance to the occupying powers, but attempts at further risings proved both short-lived and disastrous. The year 1846, especially, was destined to become a black year in Poland's history. In February the Prussian police arrested the leaders of a planned rising and the insurrection collapsed before it even began. Simultaneously the Austrian authorities, alarmed by reports of an impending rising, armed the peasants and incited them to attack the gentry. In western Galicia some two thousand patriots were killed in a massacre. In vain the highlanders in the Tatra mountains rose in arms and in the Free City of Cracow a Polish Republic was proclaimed by patriots who formed a National Government. Both the Republic and the Government lasted precisely ten days, until from the north a Russian army marched into the city. The net result of the revolt, apart from increased repression, was the incorporation of the Free City of Cracow into the Austrian Empire.

Two years later the 'Spring of Nations' in 1848 saw another attempted rising in Prussian Poland. It ended in a massacre of the insurgents. Austrian Poland was also seething, but the authorities controlled the situation with utter ruthlessness. In Cracow, for instance, though the city was quiet, the Austrian commander ordered it to be bombarded 'just in case'.

Unable to break the iron grip at home, the Poles went into battle abroad wherever there was fighting against oppression. Their most notable contribution was in Hungary, where some three thousand Poles, led by General Joseph Bem, joined in the fight for freedom and independence from Austria. Russian armed intervention brought the revolution to an end. A century later, in 1956, a mass demonstration at General Bem's statue in Budapest heralded the Hungarian rising against Stalinism.

The last great Polish insurrection of the nineteenth century broke out in Warsaw on 22nd January 1863. This time there was a more widespread and better organized conspiracy, but no Polish army to join it, as was the case in 1831. The leaders of the rising were progressive democrats, who wished to combine social reform with political freedom and national independence. As its first act the National Government of the insurgents freed the peasants and granted them the land they had been tilling. At the same time it appealed to the Lithuanian, Ukrainian and

Jewish inhabitants of the former Polish Commonwealth to rise in arms, promising them freedom and equality.

Unfortunately for the insurgents, the Tsarist authorities had anticipated this appeal with a campaign calculated to sow suspicion among the peasants and make them place their trust in the Tsar. Consequently the Ukraine failed to respond to the call to arms, but practically all Congress Poland and most of Lithuania were soon ablaze. It was largely a guerilla war, conducted with great skill and courage, but doomed to failure. As time passed and the hopes of foreign intervention failed to materialize, apart from futile British and French diplomatic protests in St. Petersburg, the Poles could see clearly that they were fighting a losing battle. Yet they fought on even after the Russians had arrested the last of the leaders and publicly hanged him in Warsaw together with four of his colleagues in August 1864.

The final shots of the rising were fired early in 1865 announcing the end of the age of Romantic Polish insurrections. At least so it seemed at the time.

11

THE ROMANTIC EMIGRATION

We have turned the name of Poland
into a prayer and a clap of thunder.
J. Slowacki

Only about eight or nine thousand people escaped from Poland to the West after the collapse of the November rising in 1831, but their importance was out of all proportion to their numbers. The Poles rightly call it the Great Emigration, because it produced an eruption of ideas and artistic talent unparalleled in Polish history.

Groups of emigrants found refuge in England, Belgium, West German States, Switzerland and the U.S.A., but by far the largest numbers gravitated to France and settled there. Suddenly Paris became the political and cultural capital of Poland. The great, free city on the Seine attracted members of the Provisional Government and Diet, university professors and journalists, poets and senior civil servants, priests and Army officers. The French Government was embarrassed by the arrival of so many 'revolutionaries', but under pressure of public opinion it gave them not only asylum but also small money allowances graded according to the former civil or military rank of the recipient.

The Ministers of Louis Philippe need not have worried about the politics of at least a substantial number of the Polish exiles. Led by Prince Adam Czartoryski, who set up his court at the Hotel Lambert in Paris, the right wing of the emigration was impeccably conservative and entertained no revolutionary ideas, working instead for the restoration of Poland through international diplomatic and military action. The rest of the emigration, however, represented every conceivable shade of liberal, radical and left-wing opinion, and each shade had its political clubs and organizations, producing a flood of leaflets, journals, pamphlets and books.

On the main objective of Poland's independence they were all agreed, but on little else. Absorbing all current new ideas, from St. Simon, to Lamennais and Hegel, arguing furiously about the past, present and future, oscillating between despair and euphoric hope and between atheistic revolt and mysticism, the Great Emigration must have appeared to an outsider like an orchestra, without a conductor.

Outstanding among this turmoil of ideas were several men of great ability and clear purposc, who tried to lead in the direction they believed to be right. But only one man came near to being recognized as the spokesman of all, and he was not a politician but a poet. His name was Adam Mickiewicz. In a fit of generosity the Parisians have even erected a monument in his memory: a huge column, surrounded by allegorical figures, supporting the statue of the poet in the flowing robes of a prophet, his left arm pointing to the sky. It is not one of Paris's most beautiful monuments. Though it stands in a prominent and central position (until recently in the place de l'Alma, now in the Cours Albert I nearby) few of the passing thousands give it even a glance and fewer still know anything about the man it honours. For outside Poland, Mickiewicz has the distinction of being probably the least well known and least read of the world's great poets.

Readers unfamiliar with the Polish language must take Mickiewicz's poetic greatness on trust, because only few fragments of his works have found translators equal to the almost impossible task. He was among the giants of the romantic period, a bold innovator who spanned the whole spectrum from the lyrical sonnet to the Olympian epic, from poetic drama to inspired, rhythmic prose. He was also a philosopher, teacher, and man of action. Mickiewicz's patriotism and his involvement with the cause of the nation have made him a spokesman of his generation and an inspirer of generation to come. But the very Polishness of his poetry created a barrier to international recognition.

Yet, in spite of his preoccupation with the fate of Poland, Mickiewicz was no narrow-minded patriot. A man of excellent classical education, a linguist whom fate made travel farther and wider than he would have wished, he also enriched Polish literature by his brilliant translations of Byron, Goethe,

Schiller, Horace, Petrarch, La Fontaine, Pushkin and others. He was a European *par excellence*, but a very Polish European.

Adam Mickiewicz was born in 1798 in or near Nowogrodek, a small town in Lithuania, then under Russian occupation, now a part of the Soviet Byelorussian Republic. His father was a lawyer, member of an impecunious gentry family who regarded themselves as Lithuanian Poles. Adam was not quite fourteen years old, a pupil in the local secondary school, when Napoleon's armies, including Polish units, marched through his native town on their way to Moscow. He was never to forget 'that spring full of longing and joyous hope', when it seemed that freedom had returned to stay.

In the year of the Congress of Vienna Mickiewicz won a scholarship to the University of Vilno, where he read classics with the view of becoming a teacher. Avidly he threw himself into the rich, stimulating and relatively free life of the Polish university, which was just passing through its most brilliant phase. He made many friends, joined secret student societies, wrote poetry and graduated in due course. In 1819 he went to Kovno (Kaunas) to teach at a secondary school, fell hopelessly in love, and published the first volume of his poems. In 1824 the Russian police discovered his membership of a secret organization and Mickiewicz was banished to Russia. He spent the next few years in St. Petersburg, Moscow and Odessa, still teaching and writing, making many new friends, among them Pushkin. From that period date his exquisite *Crimean Sonnets* and the historical poem, *Konrad Wallenrod.*

Konrad Wallenrod is an allegory on Poland's struggle with Russia, disguised as a story of Lithuania's fight against the Teutonic Knights. The hero of the poem feels that responsibility for the fate of the nation rests on his shoulders. He is a man of the highest principles, but realizes that an enslaved nation has to resort to conspiracy and deceit in order to achieve its aspirations. Wallenrod decides to sacrifice his own happiness and that of his family so that by treason and subterfuge he can destroy the enemy and save the nation.

The unsuspecting Russian censor allowed the work to be published in St. Petersburg in 1828. The following year Mickiewicz managed somehow to obtain a passport and left Russia for the West. His travels took him to Berlin, Dresden,

Prague, Weimar, then across the Alps to Florence, Rome, Naples, Pompei and back to northern Italy. But in his thoughts Mickiewicz was still in Poland, reacting to the growing wave of oppression. Surrounded by all the beauty of Italy he wrote a bitter poem addressed 'To a Polish Mother'. In it he described the fate of a young patriot, ending with these words:

> One monument of his defeat will rise:
> the gallows. And one fame he will claim his right:
> a woman weeping and wiping her eyes,
> his fellow patriots whispering through the night.[1]

By the time this poem was published in an *émigré* paper, the catastrophe of the November rising had turned a prophecy into a bitter truth. Mickiewicz himself did not take part in the rising. He made his way towards Warsaw, but when he reached the Prussian part of Poland, the capital was already under siege by the Russians. After the collapse of the insurrection Mickiewicz turned west once more, first to Dresden and finally to Paris, where he joined the ranks of the Great Emigration and soon became its prophet.

He now wrote furiously, prose, poetry and poetic drama, translations and press articles, nursed a friend dying from tuberculosis, took part in the political activities of the emigration. From that period dates his greatest work, *Pan Tadeusz*, an epic poem, which recaptures the doomed world of Polish society in Lithuania in the year of Napoleon's march on Moscow. In spite of all the anger and anguish Mickiewicz felt because of the tragic fate of his country, *Pan Tadeusz*, unlike most of his other works, is a serene epic in which, to quote another Polish poet, 'he fused *Don Quixote* with the *Iliad*.

Very little poetry came from his pen after 1834 when *Pan Tadeusz* was published. Perhaps his poetic force was spent, or the preoccupations with politics, earning a living and looking after his sick wife had sapped his inspiration. Successively Professor of Latin at the University of Lausanne and of Slavonic Literature at the Collège de France in Paris, Mickiewicz took an ever more active part in the affairs of the emigration. In 1848, when Europe appeared to be on the brink

[1] A. Mickiewicz: *Poems translated by Jack Lindsay*, Sylvan Press, London, 1957.

of a revolution, he went to Italy to organize a Polish Legion there, to fight against the Austrians. Back in Paris, he edited the radical, international paper *Tribune des Peuples*. When the Crimean War broke out he travelled to Constantinople, again trying to organize a Polish Legion. He died there of cholera in 1855.

Mickiewicz's body was brought to rest in Paris until a more liberal regime in Austria allowed it to be taken in State to Cracow and buried in the Wawel Cathedral. He was the first poet to join the kings, queens and military heroes in the Polish Pantheon.

Considering its numerical size the Great Emigration was astonishingly rich in artistic genius. Adam Mickiewicz and Frederic Chopin alone would have been enough to ensure its fame, but there were many others as well. While Chopin towered above the Polish composers and musicians of that period, Mickiewicz was surrounded by several other poets of almost equal standing. Chief among them were Julius Slowacki and Sigismund Krasinski who, together with Mickiewicz, turned the first half of the nineteenth century into the golden age of Polish poetry, reaching heights which have not been surpassed since.

If Mickiewicz was the Emigration's prophet, Slowacki was its passionate bard, endowed with a breathtaking, pyrotechnic power of words. During his short and unhappy life (1809–49) he wrote not only some of the most beautiful poetry Polish has ever known, but also the first great dramatic works to appear in the language (Shakespeare was his great influence). Like Mickiewicz he came from the eastern part of Poland (his birthplace, Krzemieniec, is now in the Soviet Ukranian Republic) and went to the University of Vilno. Poor health prevented him from fighting in the insurrection of 1830–31, but he was sent by the Provisional Government on a diplomatic mission to Paris and London. When the rising collapsed he settled first in Paris, later in Geneva.

Mickiewicz and Slowacki had much in common: intense patriotism, mysticism, a messianic vision of Poland, similar cultural influences and a certain affinity in their political outlook, yet they never became friends. Mickiewicz dismissed Slowacki's poetry as a beautiful, but soulless body; Slowacki envied the fame, and resented the awe in which the Emigration held his great rival. This stimulated him to write some of his most moving and powerful poetry, which at last, shortly before his death, won him general acclaim. In 1927 his body was taken to Cracow and placed next to Mickiewicz in the crypt of the Cathedral.

As a leading Polish authority[1] has put it, the two poets were complimentary: Mickiewicz was a sculptor with words, Slowacki was a painter and musician; Mickiewicz created a feeling of truth, Slowacki an enchanted world of his own.

The third of the poets' triumvirate was Sigismund Krasinski, a close friend of Slowacki, who came from an entirely different background. A scion of an aristocratic family, son of a General, he was born in Paris in 1812 and Napoleon was his godfather. When the 1830 rising broke out Krasinski was abroad, studying law and diplomacy at Geneva. He wanted to join the fighting but learnt that his father, the General, had thrown his lot with the Russians. Suffering tortures of remorse, young Krasinski watched the rising spread and then collapse. He never forgave his father or himself and published his works anonymously.

Burning, frustrated patriotism, combined with deep religious belief and the conviction that Poland was the Christ of nations, inspired his exquisite *Psalms*:

> All that you could, You gave us, O Lord:
> A life so pure it deserves the Cross,
> And a Cross that reaches to Your stars,
> And a mission highest of all time.

Nothing could be more Polish than those *Psalms*. Yet Krasinski was the most cosmopolitan of Polish romantics. What is perhaps his greatest work, *The Undivine Comedy*, published when he was only twenty-three years old deals with universal problems in a timeless setting. It is a prophetic play about the future social revolution, which destroys the old order and with it the old set of values, without being able to replace them by new values. As a theatrical work *The Undivine Comedy* is not a masterpiece, as a penetrating social prophecy is deserves study.

Needless to say *The Undivine Comedy* is not the favourite

[1] Juliusz Kleiner: *Zarys Dziejow Literatury Polskiej*, Wroclaw, 1964.

book among Polish communists. Partly because as a poet Krasinski did not quite measure up to Mickiewicz and Slowacki, but partly also for political reasons, this unhappy aristocrat with a conservative and pessimistic outlook has been removed from the pinnacle on which previous generations had placed him. The democrat, Mickiewicz, and the revolutionary, Slowacki, who saw 'peoples, like cranes, flying towards progress' remain secure in the official Pantheon.

Yet, Mickiewicz, Slowacki and Krasinski jointly have been the inspiration and the conscience of the unhappy, divided and enslaved nation. Their poetry became Poland's last defence.

12

NO MORE DREAMS?

All the romantic uprisings of the nineteenth century ended in tragedy for the Poles, but they achieved two things: they helped to keep the name of Poland alive and, more important still, in spite of all the quarrels and political divisions, they helped to cement the nation. In this respect the hopeless rising of 1863–64 was by far the most decisive.

When Tsar Alexander II succeeded his tyrannical father in 1855, hopes of a more liberal regime rose in his empire. In the Polish part of Russia which had lost every vestige of freedom and autonomy after the suppression of the 1830–31 rising, it seemed that a long night might be coming to an end. Indeed, there was an immediate improvement in the Congress Kingdom, but in Alexander's mind there were strict limits beyond which he was not prepared to go. He warned the Poles to give up their dreams: '*Pas des rêveries, Messieurs!*'

Some of the Poles were ready to abide by this warning and threw themselves into 'organic work' in co-operation with the Russians, improving education, building up the economy and edging towards a less oppressive regime. But the majority soon demonstrated that it was unwilling to compromise on the two essential and linked issues of freedom and independence.

When the rising erupted in January 1863, it turned out to be not only a national, but also a social revolution. On the very first day the insurgent Provisional Government issued a decree emancipating the peasants and introducing a far-reaching agrarian reform. At long last the peasants were given the land they tilled. They responded by joining the insurgent ranks in numbers greater than ever before.

Though the rising eventually collapsed under superior Russian force, the social consequences of the land reform persisted. Having quelled the rising, the Russians simply could not go back on what had happened in the villages and were forced to introduce in Congress Poland their own land reform, which confirmed most of the peasant gains and left them in a privileged position compared with their opposite numbers in Russia.

Politically the 1863 rising brought upon Poland reprisals still more savage than those that followed the 1830 insurrection. Even the name of Poland was deleted from the map when, by a decree of the Tsar, the Congress Kingdom became 'The Land on the Vistula'. An intensive drive to Russify the Poles followed.

At the same time in the Prussian part of Poland, Bismarck started a campaign to destroy the Polish character of the population and either Germanize or uproot it by all the discriminatory means at the disposal of the Berlin Government. This policy was to continue with varying intensity right up to 1914.

Only in the ailing Empire of the Hapsburgs were the Poles allowed to preserve and develop their national identity. In Galicia, as the Austrian part of Poland was called (the name was derived from that of the old Duchy of Halicz), they gained a measure of autonomy and self-government. There were Polish viceroys, an elected provincial Diet, an independent system of education with two Polish universities in Cracow and Lvov. The inhabitants of Galicia also enjoyed the right to elect Deputies to the Vienna Parliament and from among these many Austrian Ministers were recruited. On one or two occasions a Pole even held the office of the Imperial Prime Minister.

Compared with their kinsmen under the Russian and Prussian rule the Poles in Galicia had relatively little reason to complain. Their province became a haven of refuge for those who have fallen foul of the Tsarist political police and Russian revolutionaries, including Lenin himself, also found asylum there. Yet Galicia was far from being a Polish paradise. Two serious problems overshadowed the otherwise not unhappy scene.

One was the Ukrainian or Ruthenian question. While in western Galicia the Poles were in overwhelming majority, in the eastern part the opposite was true and the countryside was almost solidly Ukrainian. Only the landowners and the large towns, Lvov in particular, were predominantly Polish. Language and religion divided the Roman Catholic Poles from both the Orthodox and the Uniate Ruthenians, and the Austrians exploited these differences on the old principle of *divide at impera.*

In spite of several attempts at co-operation, the Poles and the Ruthenians remained separated from each other by a deep gulf of mistrust. Not that the Ruthenians were united; a growing sense of Ukrainian nationalism drew many of them to leaders who dreamt of an independent Ukraine, while others, inspired by ideas of religious and pan-Slav unity, gravitated towards Russia.

The other great problem of Galicia was poverty. An ill-conceived land reform after the revolutionary stirring of 1848 created a mass of poor smallholders who lived at subsistence level. At the same time the slow development of industry failed to provide work for the surplus population on the land.

By contrast in the Prussian part of Poland agriculture flourished. With a much healthier structure of land ownership introduced by the Prussians, and on much more productive land, the Poles there were prosperous and stubbornly resisted all attempts to drive them away or to turn them into good Germans. The two mainstays of this resistance were good organization (mainly in co-operative societies) and the Roman Church.

In Russian Poland the opportunities were of a different order. As the Russians dismantled Polish autonomy, they also removed barriers to trade between the Congress Kingdom and the rest of their Empire. This, and the growth of the railways, opened an enormous market for Polish industry. Result—a rapid industrialization of the Congress Kingdom, with production rising at a phenomenal rate (an average of 15 per cent per annum between 1873 and 1891). The textile industry, centred mainly on the city of Lodz, became one of the largest in Europe, while the population of Lodz itself rapidly approached the half million mark (but the city still had no municipal system of sewers). At the same time the number of towns with a population in excess of 10,000 rose from seven to twenty-six, creating a good market for the peasants.

These economic changes were at least partly due to what looked like a psychological revolution in Congress Poland. Following the collapse of the January rising, the romantic values of heroism were cast aside and the 'positivist' virtues of science, education, business and industry put in their place. The gentry ceased to despise commerce, the professional classes grew (educated mainly at the Russian Universitics of St. Petersburg and Kiev), and the industrialized cities saw growing ranks of the proletariat.

The leading Polish writer of this generation, Boleslas Prus, summed it all up in these words: 'The nation as a whole woke up, ceased to fight and conspire, and began to think and to work.' The very fact that novelists had replaced poets as national spokesmen was not without significance. From being the inspirer of heroic visions, Polish literature turned to a cool analysis of popular slogans and the dissection of national mythology. In 1886 Prus wrote:

> The Polish nation is not the Christ of nations, as the poets have told us, nor is it as bad and incompetent as our enemies would have us believe. We are . . . a young society, which has not yet found its new path of civilization. The strong hatred of the Germans testifies to its dormant strength and as for the rest, it is in the hands of God who, even in Greenland sends a joyous summer to follow the winter and northern lights. . . . We are a very young society and for that reason each of us has a little too much faith in his own views and too little respect for those of others. . . . In matters of religious conviction, national sympathies, political opinion and in our judgment of people we not only talk but we also behave as if we were infallible, in possession of the whole truth. In fact the most modest truth is like a forest in which man can only perceive the beginning of a path, and that not always clearly.

Prus was not alone in urging the Poles to change their course. Critical reassessment of the nation's aims, tactics and character became a fashion, work rather than fight became recognized as a virtue. For a short while it looked as if the Poles had settled down and reconciled themselves to their fate under the far from benevolent rule of the Tsar. The generation which had experienced the trauma of the January rising was indeed trying to rebuild and consolidate the nation on a new basis, but as the young men, for whom the fight and the repression of 1863–64 were not even a memory, came to the fore, new forces began to gather momentum—socialism and modern nationalism.

The year 1882 saw the secret formation in Warsaw of the first Polish socialist party, 'Proletariat'. This organization did not survive long under the watchful eye of the Tsarist police and in 1885 twenty-nine of its most prominent members faced trial. Among them was its leader, Ludwik Warynski, who addressed the judges in these defiant words:

> There can be no question of guilt as far as I or any of the other accused are concerned. We have fought for our convictions and we are fully justified before our consciences and before the people whose cause we have espoused. . . . We have organized the working class for a fight against the present regime. We have not been preparing a revolution, but for a revolution.

Warynski, who was sentenced to sixteen years of penal servitude and died in prison, did not mention Poland in his speech at the trial. He was an internationalist revolutionary and his attitude was representative of only one wing of Polish socialism. When the founders of the Polish Socialist Party (P.P.S.) met in Paris in 1892, they drew up a programme which linked socialism to national aspirations and stipulated the establishment of an independent Polish democratic republic.

A year later another left-wing group led by Rosa Luxemburg and Julian Marchlewski, formed a rival party under the cumbersome name of The Social Democracy of the Kingdom of Poland (S.D.K.P.). This was the beginning of the Polish communist movement, pledged to collaboration with the revolutionary forces in Russia, and opposed to Poland's independence. At first the S.D.K.P. (soon enlarged by the inclusion of Lithuania and renamed S.D.K.P. i L.) attracted considerable support, but as its anti-independence stand became clear, it found itself swimming against the nationalist tide, which favoured the P.P.S. and the newly emergent right-wing and centre parties. The socially more moderate and patriotic P.P.S., with Joseph Pilsudski as one of its leaders, eventually became the chief party of the Polish left, while the S.D.K.P. i L. contributed more to the development of communism abroad rather than inside Poland; Rosa Luxemburg became one of the leaders of German Marxism, while another prominent member of the party, Feliks Dzierzynski, ended as the man in charge of the *Cheka*, the secret police organization set up by Lenin in 1917.

The beginnings of the Polish right-wing political movement date back to the same decade which saw the emergence of socialist parties. Its theoretician and leader was the brilliant

Roman Dmowski, and the National Democratic Party (N.D.) which he founded in 1897 was destined to become one of the dominant political forces, drawing its main support from the growing ranks of the middle classes. Unashamedly nationalistic and antisemitic, Dmowski regarded Germany as Poland's chief enemy, while borrowing from the Germans the policy of 'national egoism'. Unlike the patriotic socialists, who saw Russia as the main danger, Dmowski wanted to work with the Russians for the reunification of Polish lands under the Tsar, confident that Polish superiority was such as to ensure eventual independence from St. Petersburg.

Occupying a central position in the political spectrum were the peasants who towards the end of the nineteenth century formed the Polish Peasant Party (P.S.L.), thus completing the major political alignment of the nation. But while these new movements were emerging, another and much older force was consolidating its hold over Polish loyalties: the Roman Catholic Church. Unlike in many western countries, the Church in Poland was not associated with any single political party but identified itself with the whole nation. Moreover in Prussian and Russian Poland the Church helped the people to preserve their national identity and resist the pressures of alien administrations representing other denominations, while in Galicia the Austrians deliberately exploited the religious differences between the Poles and the Ukrainians.

In this way the advent of the twentieth century saw the crystallization of the main internal forces which were to shape the destiny of Poland. Alexander's '*Pas des rêveries, Messieurs!*' had been forgotten and the Poles were again dreaming of independence, and working for it under the very noses of the occupying authorities.

Joseph Pilsudski (1867–1935), left-wing terrorist, romantic soldier, democratic first Head of resurrected Poland in 1918, dictator from 1926 till his death

Ignacy Paderewski (1860–1941), famous pianist and composer, worked for Polish independence, became Prime Minister in 1919 and President of the National Council in 1939

President Moscicki and Marshal Rydz-Smigly in 1936, the inadequate heirs to Pilsudski's power.

PART FOUR

RISE AND FALL AGAIN

13

'THE STOP CALLED INDEPENDENCE'

'Not even the extremist fancy of a café politician can imagine today how the independence of Poland could emerge from a war between the German Empire and Russia,' wrote Rosa Luxemburg in 1898. She was a highly intelligent, clear-headed marxist, but imagination was not her strong point, nor did she have much patience for nationalism. But while these words were being written, a man was already active in Poland—and nobody could accuse him of being a café politician—who was working precisely for that aim, harnessing the combined strength of the socialist and nationalist ideas. His name was Joseph Pilsudski.

Pilsudski, who was to dominate the Polish scene after the First World War (not unlike de Gaulle was to dominate the French scene after 1945), was a strange, complex and highly controversial figure, a realist with a visionary streak, probably a romantic at heart and, above all, a man of action.

Joseph Pilsudski was born in 1867, one of ten children of a Polish squire near Vilno in Polish Lithuania. He was to become a doctor, but at the University of Kharkov in the Ukraine, where he was reading medicine, he became friendly and involved with Russian revolutionaries. The Tsarist police arrested him when he was twenty and banished him to Siberia where he spent five years, graduating in the hard school of enforced exile. He returned to Poland in 1892 a confirmed socialist and patriot.

One of the founders of the P.P.S., Pilsudski was also the founder, editor, chief printer and distributor of the illegal socialist paper, *Robotnik* (*The Worker*). Moving his press from place to place in order to escape detection, Pilsudski continued to publish the paper for six years, until at last the Russian police caught up with him. They arrested him in the year 1900 and such was already his revolutionary reputation that they put him in the notorious X Pavilion of the Warsaw Citadel, from which nobody had ever succeeded in escaping. Pilsudski feigned insanity and did it so convincingly that the Russians transferred him to a military hospital in St. Petersburg. From there he escaped with relative ease and promptly resumed the publication of *Robotnik*, this time in Kiev, but soon found the Russian police on his trail once more.

Pilsudski escaped across the border into Galicia and made Cracow his headquarters. From there he travelled to London for talks with other socialists and to Tokyo, where he tried to negotiate with the Japanese Government. The outcome of this second mission illustrated the growing division between the anti-Russian P.P.S. and the pro-Russian National Democrats. The Japanese were at war with Russia and Pilsudski's objective was to obtain their help for a Polish rising in the Russian rear. He discovered, however, that Dmowski, the leader of the National Democrats, was also in Tokyo, offering quite contrary advice to the Japanese, assuring them that Pilsudski's plan was unrealistic.

The Tokyo Government refused help. Undeterred, Pilsudski returned to Cracow to plan armed resistance to the Russian call-up in the Congress Kingdom. The revolution in Russia in 1905 found a strong echo of support in Poland and Warsaw became once more the scene of demonstrations brutally suppressed by the police and the military, while in Lodz there was a short-lived armed rising. The whole country was seething with anger against the oppressive Tsarist regime and even schoolchildren went on strike for three years, demanding the right to be taught in Polish.

Pilsudski had secretly crossed the border into the Congress Kingdom and organized the fighting detachments of the P.P.S. which embarked on a campaign of terrorism against the Russians. His most famous exploit came in 1908 with the successful ambush of a mail train and the seizure of over two million roubles (about £200,000), a welcome addition to party funds. But by that time the revolutions in Russia and Poland had been suppressed, though the Tsar was forced to make concessions, and the pro-Russian National Democrats were in ascendancy. Pilsudski's own party split into two factions: P.P.S. Left Wing and P.P.S. Revolutionary Faction. The first gravitated towards Rosa Luxemburg's S.D.K.P. i L. and eventually joined it, forming the first Communist Party of Poland (K.P.P.). The second, the Revolutionary Faction, under Pilsudski's leadership, continued to fight for independence.

Once more Pilsudski had to flee from Russian-held Poland into the much freer atmosphere of Cracow, but he left a legend behind him. One of the young members of his fighting detachments, facing a Russian court martial, said: 'In my childhood dreams I saw myself as the hero, who will chase you out of here and rebuilt the Polish state.' That hero's mantle fell on Pilsudski's shoulders.

Not discouraged by the apparent hopelessness of his task, or by the opposition of the National Democrats and the conservative 'realists' of Cracow, he worked unceasingly for independence. 'Be idealistic, even romantic, in your aims, but practical and realistic in the choice of your means,' he used to say to his lieutenants. His immediate task was now the organization of the 'Riflemen's Association' in Galicia. This was to become a nucleus of Polish armed forces, for Pilsudski believed that independence would not come to Poland as a gift from foreign powers, but had to be fought for.

Early in 1914 he went to Paris to address a meeting of the French Geographical Society. He spoke of the coming war in which Poland would have to show her sword and he made the following prophetic remark: 'The problem of the independence of Poland will be definitely settled only if Russia is beaten by Germany and Germany is beaten by France. It is our duty to help to bring this about.'

When the war, which was to tear up the map of Europe drawn up at the Congress of Vienna, did eventually break out, it caught both Russia and Germany without a clear policy regarding Poland. The Russians improvised one with some haste, the Germans hesitated for a very long time. Only the Austrians knew exactly what they wanted, though for fear of upsetting their German allies did not dare to say so publicly. They wanted to unite as much of Poland as possible under the Hapsburg Crown and they thought that Pilsudski might be a useful tool in their hands. This suited Pilsudski who, regarding Russia as the chief immediate enemy, was quite willing to fight on the side of the Austrians, but on his own terms.

When war broke out Pilsudski issued a proclamation to the Polish nation:

The decisive hour has struck! Poland has ceased to be a slave and wishes to decide her own fate, her own future, throwing on the scales her own armed might. Units of the Polish Army have entered the territory of the Kingdom of Poland and are occupying it on behalf of its sole rightful owner—the Polish People....

Signed: Joseph Pilsudski,
Commander-in-Chief of the Polish Army.
Warsaw, 3rd August, 1914.

Grand words, but they were not taken seriously by the majority of the Poles. The Russians, Germans and Austrians just shrugged their shoulders and smiled. They knew that he was a long way from Warsaw; and they also knew the size of his army. Pilsudski had some 4,000 men in his Riflemen's Association in Galicia, but the Austrians, uncertain of their loyalty to the Empire, allowed him to mobilize only one company some 170 strong. At the head of this 'army' Pilsudski crossed the Russian frontier on 6th August and occupied the town of Kielce. Thus 170 men went to war against an empire of 130 millions.

A few days later Polish politicians in Galicia came to Pilsudski's rescue by forming the 'Supreme National Committee', which negotiated with the Austrians terms for the raising of Polish Legions to fight against the Russians. Pilsudski was appointed Commander of 1st Regiment of the Legions.

The Russians, in the meantime, decided to make a belated bid for Polish loyalties and the Grand Duke Nicholas, their Commander-in-Chief, issued a flowery proclamation, deploring the partitions of Poland and calling for a Polish-Russian reconciliation. Pilsudski, still regarding Russia as the first enemy, remained unmoved, but Dmowski and his National Democrats greeted the proclamation with joy. Together with three other pro-Russian parties they formed the 'Polish National Committee' in Warsaw, pledged to support the Russian war effort and started organizing Polish units to fight against the Central Powers.

At first it seemed that Dmowski was right. The Russians struck against the Austrians and penetrated deep into Galicia. The Polish Legions fought gallantly and, in spite of heavy losses, grew in numbers thanks to a continuous influex of volunteers.

Pilsudski was now a Brigadier. Then suddenly in 1915 the tide of war in Poland turned against the Russians and by the summer advancing German armies were in Warsaw. The first part of Pilsudski's prophecy was about to come true—Germany was on the point of defeating Russia—and the time had come to help to realize the second condition of Poland's independence: the defeat of Germany by the Allies. Pilsudski said so in so many words at a private meeting in Warsaw, but his remarks were greeted with amazement. His supporters pointed out that fighting Germany would be tantamount to playing the game of the Russophiles. Pilsudski retorted that in the changed circumstances of the war, a change of tactics was unavoidable. He ordered that the underground Polish Military Organization (P.O.W.) which had been set up to fight the Russians, should now turn against the Germans instead, but he judged that the time was not yet ripe for an open breach with the Central Powers.

At the end of 1915 Austria and Germany publicly dashed any Polish hopes as to their role in restoring independence by dividing between them the Congress Kingdom, the whole of which was now in their hands. Pilsudski reacted by resigning his commission in the Legions and returned as a private citizen to Cracow. His example was followed by the majority of the Legionaries, who demanded permission to withdraw from the fighting; the Austrians had no choice but to comply.

Soon, however, the toll of the fighting on the Western Front drew the German High Command to the reluctant conclusion that they needed a Polish army fighting on their side and that it it was worth making at least vague concessions to Polish national demands in order to secure a fresh supply of cannon fodder. The Generals argued that if some kind of a Polish State was set up, they could count on 800,000 new recruits from the Congress Kingdom. Distasteful as the idea was to most German politicians, the Central Powers proclaimed on 5th November 1916 the creation of 'an independent Kingdom of Poland' without defining its precise status or territory.

When this vague gesture brought no rush of Poles to the recruiting offices, the Germans and the Austrians set up in Warsaw a 'Polish Council of State' composed of twenty-five members. Pilsudski was one of them and he was put in charge of an embryonic Ministry of War.

This arrangement was unlikely to last. Soon Pilsudski was at loggerheads with the Germans about the terms on which a Polish army was to be raised. Under his influence the Council of State refused to issue a general call to arms until the terms were settled to their satisfaction. When the Germans insisted that all Polish soldiers take an oath binding them to 'fidelity in arms' with the German and Austrian forces, Pilsudski resigned from the Council and all the other left-wing members followed suit.

A private citizen once more, he devoted himself to the strengthening of the secret P.O.W. This activity did not escape the notice of the German police; he was arrested in July 1917 together with his Chief of Staff, Casimir Sosnkowski, and imprisoned in the fortress of Magdeburg. The remaining members of the Council of State resigned in protest.

But the German need for a Polish army continued to grow. In September 1917 the Central Powers announced the setting up in Warsaw of a Regency Council composed of the Mayor of the capital (Prince Lubomirski), a wealthy landowner (Count Ostrowski) and the Archbishop of Warsaw. The Regents in turn appointed a Government, which started to organize a civil administration, but they enjoyed neither the support of the pro-Russian right nor of the Pilsudski-led left. At that stage, however, the outbreak of the Bolshevik revolution suddenly played into their hands. The National Democrats finally had to abandon hope of restoring Polish independence in collaboration with the Russians, and Polish units in Russia started fighting the Bolsheviks, some of them even entering into an informal alliance with the Germans.

The treaties of Brest Litovsk with the Ukrainian Republic and with Russia, put an abrupt end to this short-lived co-operation. Not only had the Germans established a Kingdom of Lithuania under their own protection and supported an independent Ukrainian Republic, but they even forced the Austrians to promise to surrender eastern Galicia to the Ukrainians. In the eyes of the Poles this was final proof that the Germans had no intention of restoring a geuinely independent Poland within acceptable frontiers.

The Council of Regents made a futile protest against 'this new partition of Poland', there were demonstrations in the streets of Warsaw, the remainder of the Legions declared itself freed from their oath of allegiance to the Austrian Emperor and tried to fight their way to Polish units in Russia, only to be forcibly disarmed by the Germans. As far as Poland was concerned the Central Powers' policy was in ruins. Fortunately for the Poles the days of the Central Powers themselves were numbered.

Austria was the first to crumble and during the night of 6th November 1918 the secret P.O.W., led by one of Pilsudski's closest lieutenants, Rydz-Smigly, struck in Lublin, disarmed the Austrians, and set up a Provisional People's Government of the Polish Republic. The head of this government was Pilsudski's old political ally, the leader of the P.P.S. in Galicia, Ignacy Daszynski, and the post of Minister of Defence was kept vacant for Pilsudski himself. In a proclamation to the people the Provisional Government declared itself to be the sole legal authority for the whole of Poland, pending the election of a Diet, promised far-reaching social reforms and absolute equality of all nationalities, races and religions.

Thus on the eve of the armistice Poland had two Governments and it looked as if the long awaited independence might begin with civil war. At this stage fate intervened; the republican revolution in Germany resulted in the release of Pilsudski from the Magdeburg fortress. He arrived in Warsaw on 11th November. The long imprisonment helped to turn the former socialist-terrorist and leader of the Legions into a national hero who enjoyed the respect of even his bitter political enemies. At the railway station he was greeted by one of the Regents, Prince Lubomirski, and drove through the streets filled with cheering crowds.

The Council of Regency appointed him Commander-in-Chief. Three days later, yielding to popular pressure, the Regents resigned in favour of Pilsudski, who became Head of State while retaining the supreme military command. The Lublin Provisional Government dissolved itself and Pilsudski called Daszynski to Warsaw, to become the first Prime Minister of the Independent Republic. This was greeted with such outcry by the right that Pilsudski immediately replaced him by Moraczewski, a much more moderate socialist, who succeeded in forming the first coalition Cabinet. National unity was now Pilsudski's aim and he was not prepared to allow his long socialist past to tie his hands in the choice of men or means. 'We have travelled a long way together,' he told his old political associates, 'but I've got out at the stop called Independence.'

But the achievement of national unity seemed as unlikely as the solution of a host of other problems, which were advancing in battalions on Pilsudski's Poland. He was at the head of a country with no frontiers, no effective central administration, no army and no treasury. Not a single government in the world recognized him. Most of Poland was still occupied by the Germans, while Polish army units which had sprung up during the last phase of the war were either in France or scattered all over Russia. Poor, devastated by war, hungry and far from united, the infant state was in danger of drowning in general chaos.

14

WHAT SORT OF POLAND?

The end of the First World War left a power vacuum in central and eastern Europe. The three Empires which had carved up Poland in the eighteenth century were themselves in ruins. Germany, bled white by the war, faced turmoil under its new and uncertain republican government; Russia, convulsed by the Bolshevik revolution, was torn by civil war; the Austro-Hungarian Empire of the Hapsburgs had disintegrated altogether. What sort of Poland would emerge from all this chaos? The answer to this question was of vital importance not only to the Poles themselves, but to the future peace of Europe.

The head of the new Polish Republic, Joseph Pilsudski, knew exactly the kind of Poland he wanted to build. This former socialist, who was a romantic realist, envisaged the resurrection of the Jagiellonian Commonwealth in the modern form of a federation of Poland, the Ukraine, Lithuania and possibly also the other Baltic states. He was prepared to grant autonomy to each constituent nation, with Poland as the strongest, exercising through its culture a unifying influence over the whole of the federation. He set about building a United States of Central Europe, but the odds were against him.

Pilsudski was in charge of Warsaw, but he was far from being the undisputed ruler of Poland proper, not to mention the other countries which used to belong to the Jagiellonian Commonwealth. Practically the whole of eastern Galicia was in the hands of Ukrainian nationalists, with only a small Polish garrison holding out in the city of Lvov. A German-sponsored nationalist government in Kaunas raised the standard of Lithuanian independence, while in Minsk a Soviet Government of Lithuania and White Russia had its eyes firmly fixed on Moscow. The frontiers with Germany and Czechoslovakia were not yet drawn and, more important still, the whole of the formerly German province of Poznan had declared its allegiance not to Pilsudski but to his great rival, the right-wing leader, Roman Dmowski. To complicate matters further, the victorious Allies recognized Dmowski's Polish National Committee in Paris as the legal representative of the Polish nation and they viewed Pilsudski with the greatest suspicion.

Dmowski and his National Committee, dominated by the National Democrats, wanted Poland to become a strong, centralized state, with frontiers extended far west at the expense of Germany. The Allies themselves were committed to the establishment of an independent Poland in accordance with the principles of self-determination, without realizing how difficult, if not impossible, it would be to find clear ethnographic frontiers in central Europe. Lloyd George had gone on record 'that independent Poland, comprising all those genuinely Polish elements who desire to form part of it, is an urgent necessity for the stability of Western Europe' (8th January 1918). President Wilson in the thirteenth of his Fourteen Points stated: 'An independent Polish state should be erected, which should include the territories inhabited by indisputably Polish populations, which should be assured a free and secure access to the sea, and whose political and economic independence and territorial integrity should be guaranteed by international covenant.'

Thus soon after the Armistice three conflicting concepts came into play. The Allied statesmen wanted to set up a relatively small Polish state, comprising only those lands where the Poles were in a majority, though with a guaranteed access to the sea; Dmowski and his National Committee claimed for Poland her pre-partition frontiers plus Upper Silesia and East Prussia with the aim of creating a powerful unitarian state, which could become a bulwark against German expansion; Pilsudski aimed at transforming the former Jagiellonian Commonwealth into a great federation, capable of standing up to both Russian and German imperialism.

As long as the Poles remained divided, neither Pilsudski nor Dmowski had much chance of achieving their aims. However, an alliance between the two implied at least a temporary compromise regarding the ultimate character of Poland. Pilsudski saw this clearly and made early overtures to the National Committee in Paris, but Dmowski ignored them. It needed an intervention by the third outstanding Pole of that generation to bring about a semblance of unity. His name was Paderewski.

Ignacy Paderewski, the world-famous pianist and composer, had campaigned vigorously for the Polish cause in the United States during the war. Largely under his influence President Wilson, even before America entered the war, had committed his country to creating an independent Poland and Paderewski's prestige among the Poles was enormous. When the Allies formally recognized the National Committee in Paris, Paderewski became its envoy in Washington. But in December 1918 he travelled to Europe and, after talks with Dmowski in Paris, proceeded on board a British warship to Gdansk. In Poland he was given a hero's welcome wherever he went. At the beginning of January he met Pilsudski for the first time; a few days later the Head of State dismissed the socialist Premier Moraczewski, and entrusted Paderewski with the mission of forming a Government of National Unity.

Dmowski had no choice but to recognize Paderewski's Government. Pilsudski in return formally agreed to the National Committee in Paris acting on Poland's behalf in the West, but he introduced into it a few men on whose loyalty he could count. Temporarily at least the Poles were united to face the overwhelming difficulties of establishing their young state.

At the Peace Conference in Paris Dmowski (who was later joined by Paderewski) had to fight a hard battle for Poland's western frontiers, while simultaneously in Warsaw Pilsudski had the task of turning the disorganized fragments of three Empires into a cohesive state and trying to come to terms with his eastern neighbours. Neither Pilsudski nor Dmowski could claim unqualified success. In spite of Dmowski's eloquence and persistence, backed by volumes of historical and statistical evidence, the Western Allies would not agree to his ambitious demands. With the exception of the French they neither wanted to weaken Germany unduly, nor did they want to include large numbers of Germans in the new Polish state. The Poles would only get these territories where they were in a majority. In cases of doubt, in the border districts of East Prussia and in Upper Silesia, the issue would be decided by plebiscite. Having promised Poland a free access to the sea, the Allies gave her a part of eastern Pomerania with a minute Baltic coastline and no single port of significance; the historically Polish port of Gdansk, whose inhabitants were almost a hundred per cent German, became a Free City under the League of Nations.

In the east Pilsudski tried to exploit the fluid situation and entice the Lithuanians and Ukrainians into a federation with Poland, but he underestimated both the strength of their new nationalism and the gulf which still existed between the Polish landowners and townspeople on the one hand and the Lithuanian, White Russian and Ukrainian peasants on the other. His call for a federation fell on deaf ears of the nationalist middle classes, while in the countryside the Bolsheviks could always outbid him by making more lavish promises to the peasants at the expense of the landlords. Only in the case of the nationalist government of the eastern Ukraine under Petljura the twin dangers of the Bolsheviks and Denikin's White army made the Ukrainians seek an alliance with Poland and agree in principle to a federal union.

Pilsudski's policy towards the Bolsheviks looked ambivalent, but there was logic behind it. He refused to intervene on the side of the Whites, knowing full well that both Denikin and Kolchak were Russian imperialists of the old school opposed to Poland expanding beyond the frontiers of the former Congress Kingdom, but he also mistrusted Bolshevik intentions.

During the year 1919, while Dmowski and Paderewski argued the Polish case in Paris, Pilsudski consolidated the state, built up an administration and an army, reconquered eastern Galicia from the nationalist forces of the ephemeral West Ukrainian Government, and negotiated simultaneously with the Reds and the Whites, with the Ukrainians under Petljura and with the newly emergent Baltic States. At the same time Pilsudski's forces advanced cautiously against the Bolsheviks in the Soviet Lithuanian and White Russian Republic, until the front was stabilized on a line running east of the city of Minsk.

The Western Allies, though they were really powerless to settle the Polish-Soviet frontier, tried to prevent Poland from incorporating the former eastern marshes of the Jagiellonian Commonwealth, so as not to alienate the anti-communist Russians. On 8th December 1919 the Supreme Council of the Allies fixed a provisional administrative eastern frontier of Poland along a line roughly following that of the eastern frontier of the former Congress Kingdom; the future of eastern Galicia was left undecided. Though the Allies expressly reserved Poland's right to establish claims to territories east of the provisional frontiers, Dmowski protested violently against this announcement.

Meanwhile Pilsudski had taken matters into his own hands. At the end of November, dissatisfied with Lenin's evasive answers, he broke off negotiations with the Bolsheviks and, together with the Latvians, attacked on the northern front, along the River Dvina, capturing the fortress of Dvinsk. The Russians reacted with a fresh peace proposal on terms very generous to Poland. They offered to cede large parts of Byelorussia and the Ukraine, in fact everything west of the existing front line. This would have established Poland's boundary more than half way between that of the former Congress Kingdom and the 1772 frontier. We will never know how genuine this offer was. Pilsudski suspected that it was not, that Lenin had made it purely to gain time and allow the Red Army to finish off the Whites before turning against Poland. He insisted that the peace talks should take place in the town of Borissov, right on the front line; the Bolsheviks offered to negotiate anywhere but at Borissov. This, combined with intelligence reports of Red Army concentrations behind the front line, made Pilsudski decide to strike first. In spite of Allied warnings that he would get help only if Poland was attacked within her ethnographic frontiers, he ordered an advance into the Ukraine.

Under the command of General Rydz-Smigly Polish and Ukrainian divisions started to advance on 25th April 1920. Within a fortnight Kiev was in their hands. Pilsudski, now a Marshal of Poland, was hailed as a conquering hero and the vision of Poland restored to pre-1772 frontiers suddenly seemed within grasp. Joyous *Te Deum* resounded in all Polish churches and even the National Democrats grudgingly joined in the praise of Pilsudski. But the rejoicing was premature.

A week after the Polish entry into Kiev the Red Army under General (later Marshal) Tukhachevsky attacked on the Byelorussian front, and on 8th June Soviet cavalry under Budienny broke through the Polish lines south of Kiev. By the end of July the Russians were once more at the gates of Warsaw and the

Polish army was reeling under the hammer blows from the east. A communist 'Provisional Government of Poland' was set up in Bialystok and Tukhachevsky announced in an order of the day that 'over the corpse of Poland leads the way to universal conflagration'.

There was panic in Warsaw. Pilsudski later wrote: 'The sight of these threatening storm clouds was shaking the state, weakening peoples' characters, softening the resolution of soldiers' hearts.'[1] But Pilsudski himself kept a cool head. He needed to. Panic was not confined to Warsaw. The Western Allies, alarmed by the prospect of a Bolshevik advance into the heart of Europe, demanded that Poland sued for peace on the basis of the line drawn by the Supreme Council on 8th December 1919 and now extended across Galicia—this line later became known as the Curzon line and has been much quoted by the Soviet Union in justification of Russian territorial claims on Poland.

While a Polish Government delegation was trying to reach Tukhachevsky's headquarters at Minsk to negotiate an armistice, Pilsudski was planning the Battle of Warsaw. He disregarded the advice of an Allied military mission under General Weygand and decided to counter attack even before the envoys left Warsaw. By the time the negotiations at Minsk began, his counter offensive was under way. The Polish delegation found the Russian terms exceedingly harsh: not only was the frontier to follow the Curzon line, but the future Polish army was to be limited to 50,000 men, Allied military missions were to leave Warsaw and the Polish arms industry was to be dismantled. By the time the Russians had spelled out these terms, which would have left Poland at the mercy of Moscow, the Red Army was already in retreat that quickly turned into a rout. Pilsudski's plan succeeded beyond even his wildest dreams and within a month the Poles were again in possession of Minsk, having won what Lord d'Abernon described as 'the eighteenth decisive battle of the world'.

The next round of Polish-Soviet peace talks held in Riga produced agreement and a peace treaty which came into force on 30th April 1921. The Poles, though victorious, showed certain moderation. They accepted a frontier considerably less

[1] J. Pilsudski: *Rok 1920*, Warsaw, 1924.

World War II. In the West a Polish Government-in-exile under General Sikorski (*right*) continued the fight. In Poland itself resistance was fierce and Nazi repression knew no bounds, as the ruins of the Warsaw Ghetto testify (*below*)

The Communist rulers of Poland, Edward Ochab (*top left*) held the reins of power just before Ladislas Gomulka (*top right*) took over during the "Spring in October" of 1956. Joseph Cyrankiewicz, Prime Minister since 1954, has travelled far and wide. The photograph below shows him (*centre*) with Gomulka (*right*) flanking Ulbricht during a visit to East Berlin

favourable than that offered by the Russians in January 1920 and they withdrew from Minsk and several other towns. However, the new frontier gave them over 40,000 square miles of territory east of the Allied line of 8th December, plus eastern Galicia, with a mixed population of whom the Poles were the largest national group, representing about one-third of the total.

There remained the question of Vilno and district, which the Russians had ceded to Lithuania, and of Upper Silesia where a plebiscite was to decide the frontier. Pilsudski had strong views about Vilno, his native city, which he regarded as Polish and was not prepared to allow it to go to Lithuania. Nor did he want to fight a war with the small Lithuanian state. On his secret orders General Zeligowski, at the head of a division composed of soldiers from the Vilno region, occupied the city ostensibly in defiance of the Polish Government and set up a provisional military administration there. Only later was Vilno formally incorporated into Poland.

The plebiscites in East Prussian districts, held during the Soviet advance on Warsaw, had produced results unfavourable to Poland, and the old frontier was allowed to stand. Much more important, however, was the plebiscite which was still to take place in the rich industrial region of Upper Silesia. Originally Polish under Piast princes, this province had been subjected to centuries of German influence and the outcome of the plebiscite was very much in doubt. In an attempt to force the issue the P.O.W. organized two Polish armed risings, which were however suppressed. At last, on 20th March 1921, under international supervision, the people of Silesia went to the polls. The result was disappointing from the Polish point of view—only just over 40 per cent of the people voted for incorporation into Poland, while nearly 60 per cent declared themselves in favour of Germany. A third Polish rising followed and for more than a month there was bloody fighting in Silesia. Eventually the Council of the League of Nations arranged a division of Silesia, assigning to Poland that part where a majority had opted against Germany. This included the important city of Katowice and a large part of the mining and industrial area.

Finally, the delimitation of the Polish-Czechoslovak frontier on a sector adjoining Silesia also caused a great deal of bad blood, though without actual fighting. Both sides claimed most of the former Duchy of Teschen. In January 1919 Czech troops occupied the western part of the disputed territory. The Poles protested. The Supreme Allied Council tried to arrange a plebiscite, but this came to nothing and eventually an Inter-Allied Commission divided the Duchy, giving Czechoslovakia the larger and more valuable part of the province, including a part of the town of Teschen itself. The Poles protested again and the dispute was not settled until 1924, when the Poles finally, but grudgingly, accepted the Inter-Allied award.

Thus the Polish state, which emerged from the ruins left by the First World War, was a compromise creation. It was a large country of some 150,000 square miles (much larger than the United Kingdom) with a population of about 27 million, of whom only about two-thirds were Poles. The rest of the population consisted of some four million Ukrainians, nearly three million Jews, about one million each of Germans and Byelorussians, and smaller numbers of Russians. Lithuanians, Tartars and so on. In this way Poland was a multi-nation state, but both in size and in concept it fell far short of Pilsudski's idea of a federal commonwealth, for the Diet, largely under the influence of Dmowski's National Democrats, gave Poland a unitarian constitution, modelled largely on that of the French Third Republic. This constitution enshrined all the principles of parliamentary democracy, all political and religious freedoms, but it made no provision for regional autonomy, nor did it make any allowances for the Poles' lack of experience in this, or for that matter any other form of government.

Since, according to the Constitution, the President of the Republic was reduced to the role of a mere figure-head, Pilsudski would not allow his own name to go forward as Presidential candidate. On 14th December 1922 he handed over his seal of office to the first elected President of the Republic, Professor Gabriel Narutowicz, who on taking his oath declared that he would follow faithfully Pilsudski's policy of 'peace, justice and impartiality towards all Polish citizens without distinction of origin or opinion'. Two days later Narutowicz was assassinated.

15

PILSUDSKI'S POLAND

Admirers of Marshal Pilsudski have regarded him as the saviour of Poland and his country's greatest son. His opponents have called him a fascist dictator and a bloody tyrant who led his country to disaster. Neither description is accurate, though both contain elements of truth. Joseph Pilsudski, the absolute ruler of Poland between 1926 and 1935, defies precise classification. He was certainly no fascist dictator in the style of Hitler or Mussolini. If anything, one might perhaps call him the Polish de Gaulle, for there are some striking similarities between the roles of the two men.

Both Pilsudski and de Gaulle led their countries' armed struggle for freedom and came to power at the end of a world war; both relinquished power in protest against the constitutional weakness of the executive, and retired into private life, only to return to the helm later (by different methods), when their country was threatened by chaos, to rule thereafter in a more or less absolute manner. Both had romantic visions about the historic role of their countries and excelled in realistic diplomacy, while sharing a strong contempt for professional politicians.

Pilsudski, who relinquished the office of Head of State when the new Constitution, largely modelled on that of the French Third Republic, came into force towards the end of 1922, watched with dismay the development of Polish democracy. The system of proportional representation combined with Polish individualism was guaranteed to produce Parliaments without a clear majority, and incapable of forming a stable government. The strongest party in the Seym were Pilsudski's sworn enemies, the right-wing National Democrats, led by Roman Dmowski. Together with their allies they held 163 out of the 444 parliamentary seats. The centre of the spectrum was occupied by two peasant parties with the joint strength of 119 seats, but constantly at loggerheads with each other. On the left the P.P.S., Pilsudski's former party, had only 41 seats. There were 34 deputies from a variety of minor parties and the balance in Parliament was held by 87 deputies representing national and religious minorities—Germans, Jews, Ukrainians and Byelorussians. It was the vote of the national minorities which decided the outcome of the election of the first President Gabriel Narutowicz, against the candidate of the right, Count Zamoyski. To men of the extreme right this amounted to national humiliation and drove one of them to murder the President only two days after he took office.

Parliament elected another man of the left, Stanislas Wojciechowski, as President of the Republic, but within a few months the National Democrats became the senior partners in a coalition government; Pilsudski relinquished his remaining military appointments and retired to the country. Unstable governments followed each other (between November 1918 and May 1926 Poland had fifteen different governments with an average life span of five months). The economic situation deteriorated, with inflation reducing the value of the currency until fifteen million Polish marks could not buy one U.S. dollar. Strikes were frequent and threatened to cripple the weak economy. . . . The political climate was harsh and bitter, administration inefficient and corrupt, minorities dissatisfied. A drastic currency reform in 1924 restored the economic situation for the time being, but by the following year the new unit of currency, the zloty was sliding down once more, unemployment rose sharply and the Government adopted strong deflationary measures. This led to the break up of the coalition, rioting by the unemployed and a protracted government crisis.

Pilsudski watched the continuing parliamentary and administrative chaos with anxiety mixed with contempt. He had never had much patience for professional politicians and their performance since he withdrew from office confirmed his worst fear—the Polish streak of anarchy was about to reassert itself. On 12th May 1926 he intervened by force of arms. In spite of a systematic campaign of denigration conducted against him by the National Democrats, and in spite of the replacement of his supporters in key military posts by his opponents, Pilsudski's influence in the army was still enormous. At the head of several regiments loyal to him he marched on Warsaw and occupied it after two days' fighting. A general strike proclaimed by the P.P.S. prevented government reinforcements from reaching the capital; by 15th May both the Government and the President of the Republic had resigned.

The National Assembly (the Seym and Senate in joint session) met to choose a new President of the Republic. It elected Pilsudski on the first ballot with a majority of 99 votes over the candidate of the Right. In a courteous letter Pilsudski declined the office which, he said, was too circumscribed by the Constitution to allow its holder to take effective action. He was grateful, however, for the vote of support which had legalized his *coup*. The Assembly met again and on the second ballot elected Ignacy Moscicki, a friend of the Marshal and a distinguished professor of chemistry. Another of Pilsudski's supporters became Prime Minister, while the Marshal himself was satisfied with the post of Minister of Defence and held the reins of real power behind the scenes.

What did Pilsudski want to achieve? In an interview published in a Paris newspaper he said:

> I am a strong man and I like to decide all matters by myself. When I consider the history of my country, I cannot really believe that Poland can be governed by the stick. I don't like the stick. . . . No, I am not in favour of a dictatorship in Poland. I conceive the role of the Chief of State in a different fashion—it is necessary that he should have the right to make quick decisions on questions of national interest. The chicanes of Parliament retard indispensable solutions. The authority of the President must be increased. . . . A great effort of honesty is needed after the demoralization caused by the years of war and the centuries of slavery. I have friends in the Right and in the Left, but Poland cannot recover on a policy of a party—the country and myself have had enough of these labels and programmes.[1]

Pilsudski's return to power was greeted with acclaim by the Left and by the national minorities. Both expected from him more fairness, humanity with justice and stability combined with efficiency. Pilsudski was to disappoint most of these hopes. At fifty-nine he was already an old man, impatient, brusque, even brutal in his dealings with opponents, yet nobody could

[1] Quoted in Robert Machray: *The Poland of Pilsudski*, London, 1936.

doubt his motives and his own austere, almost ascetic integrity.

In spite of what he said in the interview he did become dictator of Poland in all but name, and he did use the stick. Twice he held the office of Prime Minister, but he disliked it since this involved dealing with Parliament, which he described as 'the House of Prostitutes', and he preferred to exercise power through his nominees, while remaining Minister of Defence. He surrounded himself with men whose loyalty he could trust, most of them old comrades from the Legions, who owed their promotion to him. This was the so-called Regime of the Colonels. There were among them some very able men, but also many unequal to the tasks he had assigned to them; none of his lieutenants had the ability or stature either to stand up to Pilsudski or to succeed him.

Like de Gaulle more than twenty years later, Pilsudski also tried to form a non-party block of supporters in Parliament. When this failed to achieve the necessary majority in Parliament, the Marshal, unlike de Gaulle, broke the opposition by force. He had the leaders of a centre-left coalition of parties arrested and sent to the fortress of Brest Litovsk where they were maltreated. Later some of them were brought to trial on charges of conspiring to overthrow the Government; the judges, by a majority of five to one, found them guilty, but imposed only short sentences of imprisonment. Finally, like de Gaulle again, Pilsudski had the constitution changed for one of the presidential type, but unlike de Gaulle he did not live to see it come into force. On 12th May 1935, precisely nine years after the *coup d'état*, the President of the Republic, Ignacy Moscicki issued a proclamation to the people:

> Marshal Joseph Pilsudski has died.
>
> By the great labour of his life he built up strength in the Nation, by his genius of mind and hard effort of will he resuscitated the State. He led it towards rebirth of its own power, towards emancipation of forces on which the future strength of Poland will be based. . . .[1]

With great pomp and circumstance Pilsudski was laid to rest in the crypt of the Wawel Cathedral in Cracow, next to Poland's kings, poets and famous leaders of the fight for independence.

[1] Quoted in Robert Machray: *The Poland of Pilsudski*, London, 1936.

Among the distinguished foreign representatives who walked behind his coffin, was Field Marshal Hermann Goering, whose Luftwaffe was to bury Pilsudski's Poland only four years later.

Though by no means all agreed with Moscicki's assessment of the late dictator, the death of Pilsudski almost united the nation in mourning the man who had become something of a father figure. For all his mistakes (and they were many) he had towered like a giant over his contemporaries and his services to the country had been enormous. The rise of Nazi terror in Germany and of Stalinist terror in the Soviet Union had also brought home to the Poles that the Pilsudski's regime, in spite of all its repressive measures, had been relatively liberal and under him Poland had continued to enjoy at least a certain degree of political freedom; the opposition parties, once their power had been broken, were allowed to continue, with none of their leaders having to live in fear of their lives; the press, though subject to censorship, could criticize; the people could speak their minds quite freely.

Pilsudski's greatest mistakes were in the field of internal policy. He destroyed parliamentary democracy without producing a viable alternative to it. His vision of a federal state having come to nothing, he allowed the National Democrat policy of 'Polonization' of the minorities to continue and when the Ukrainians in east Galicia showed resistance, this was suppressed with great and unnecessary ferocity. Though not an anti-semite, he allowed antisemitism to spread. Though a former socialist, he allowed a drastic policy of deflation to continue, bringing hardship and unemployment. He did not press the much needed agrarian reform with sufficient vigour. Against all this he could claim credit for introducing a continuity and stability of government which helped to consolidate the country, develop the economy, build up the educational system, advancing Poland slowly but unmistakably.

It was in the field of foreign affairs that his greatest achievement lay. Pilsudski saw clearly that Poland could not survive surrounded by hostile neighbours, with distant France and weak Rumania as her only allies. He set out to establish normal relations all round, especially with Germany and the Soviet Union. This was no easy task. The Germans stubbornly remained hostile, but the Russians were at least prepared to talk. From 1926 until 1932 negotiations continued on and off until on 25th July 1932 Poland and the Soviet Union signed in Moscow a three-year non-aggression pact.

When Hitler came to power, and not only subscribed to the policy of revising the frontier with Poland but also started re-arming in secret, Pilsudski, who had an excellent intelligence network in Germany, saw the red light and wanted to act. Repeatedly he suggested to the French a joint 'preventive action', with the aim of compelling Germany to observe the provisions of the Treaty of Versailles. When it became clear that the French would do nothing, Pilsudski decided to parley with Hitler. The Polish approach to Berlin was welcome as it came at a moment when Hitler was preparing to put an end to German-Soviet co-operation. On 26th January 1934 a Polish-German ten-year non-agression pact was signed and for the first time in living memory the relations between the two countries became normal.

This did not mean that Pilsudski would join Hitler in his anti-communist crusade. The dangers of this were obvious to him and he started negotiating with the Russians for a non-aggression treaty of similar duration. This was signed on 5th May 1934, replacing the previous short-term Polish-Soviet agreement. In this way Pilsudski did all he could to ensure Poland's international recognition and stability, while preserving neutrality towards her two powerful neighbours.

But Poland was neither small enough to become the Switzerland of central Europe, nor had her neighbours ever given up their claims to large parts of Polish territory. She needed both to be strong herself and to have powerful allies who could come to her rescue. While Pilsudski was alive, he was careful to cultivate the alliance with France, while building up the Polish army to the limit of the country's resources. He knew, however, that Poland, with her predominantly agricultural economy, and a primitive one at that, and a national income per head among the lowest in Europe, could never match the strength of Germany or Russia.

Already in 1932 Pilsudski saw the coming break-up of the post-war system. On 2nd November, when asking Colonel Joseph Beck to take over the Foreign Ministry, he said to him: '. . . times are coming when the conventional structure of international life, which has endured almost throughout the past ten years, will be shaken. Forms which the world has become accustomed to regard as permanent are crumbling to pieces. . . . This development will be accompanied by a series of prolonged complications, and we in Poland will have to face, as time goes on, the problem of standing up for Poland's views, perhaps against everybody. . . . But remember above all that you must not entertain ideas and plans that exceed the capacity of the instrument which has to carry it out. . . .'[1]

Wise words, but could adherence to this realistic prescription save Poland? It is clear now that once Hitler and Stalin had jointly decided to wipe Poland off the map, no Polish policy and no power on earth could avert disaster. In the event, after the death of Pilsudski, the Poles had only mediocre men to guide them, and the Marshal's successors followed a policy which helped Hitler in his work of destruction.

There was no one man who could step into Pilsudski's shoes and three of his chief lieutenants became effectively the joint heirs to his power: President Moscicki, General Rydz-Smigly and Colonel Beck. Ignacy Moscicki, a former professor of chemistry, made a handsome and distinguished-looking Head of State; he may have been a brilliant scientist, but he lacked political genius. General Edward Rydz-Smigly, an excellent commander in the field, was neither a strategist, nor a politician, yet it was he who by virtue of his control of the Army became the strong man of the regime. Colonel Joseph Beck was the flexible, opportunist Foreign Minister, and the third member of the unofficial triumvirate in charge of the destiny of Poland.

Ostensibly Beck followed the course set by Pilsudski, but he committed two grave mistakes: he over-estimated Poland's power and, by pursuing short-term objectives, he helped to compromise her long-term interests. He wanted his country to play a great-power role at the head of an alliance of states stretching from the Baltic to the Black Sea and the Adriatic. The idea of such an alliance had some attraction only for the Rumanians and the Hungarians, but the Czechs and Lithuanians would not hear of it, while the Yugoslavs remained on the fence. Beck allowed his frustration and the Polish grievance about Teschen to blur his judgment; failing to see the danger to

[1] Quoted in J. H. Hartley and C. Wrzos: *Colonel Beck*, London, 1939.

Poland, he helped Hitler to destroy Czechoslovakia during and after the Munich crisis, by raising Poland's claim to Teschen and annexing it in October 1938. This gave Poland a small, industrially important district, but the price she had to pay for it was high: when Hitler finally marched into Czechoslovakia his troops surrounded Poland not only from the north and the west, but also from the south.

And Poland was obviously next on Hitler's agenda of conquest. At that stage Beck showed courage. He gratefully accepted Chamberlain's guarantee of the integrity of the Polish state (31st March 1939) and negotiated the British-Polish treaty of mutual assistance. Hitler replied by denouncing the Polish-German non-agression pact. But whatever his past mistakes, Beck was not going to capitulate to Hitler. 'We in Poland,' he said in a speech to the Seym on 5th May 1939, 'do not know the concept of peace at any price. There is only one thing in the life of men, nations and States which is above price—and that is honour.'

For once the whole nation was behind its government. But the doom of Pilsudski's Poland was only a matter of weeks and Beck's brave words became her epitaph.

16

HITLER AND THE POLES

> No arts; no letters; no society;
> and which is worst of all: continual
> fear and danger of violent death;
> and the life of man, solitary, poor,
> nasty, brutish and short.
>
> Thomas Hobbes: *Leviathan*

At dawn on 1st September 1939, when Hitler launched his armed might on Poland, he not only unleashed a world war, but he opened an indescribably horrible chapter of German-Polish relations. What the Germans did in Poland between 1939 and 1944 was in its calculated evil and brutality so far in excess of the Nazi misdeeds in the West that it will take generations before Polish memories of this monstrous period and the fear and hatred of Germany can fade away.

The September campaign in Poland was only a mild foretaste of things to come. The world had its first demonstration of Hitler's *Blitzkrieg*, of total war involving soldiers and civilians alike. All the advantages were on Hitler's side: geography, numbers, arms and strategy. He had the choice of where to strike—his forces surrounded Poland from three sides—East Prussia in the north, Germany proper in the west and the rump of Czechoslovakia in the south. He also had the choice of when to strike.

Though the portents were clear enough, Poland, following the advice of her Western Allies who still subscribed to the theory that 'Hitler must not be provoked', was not yet fully mobilized. The Polish General Staff had a difficult choice of alternative plans: to try the impossible and defend the whole 1,500 or so miles of the frontier, or to withdraw behind the line of the Vistula, surrendering the most important industrial regions and access to the sea. They chose to try the impossible.

The campaign followed an easily predictable course. Courage

and cavalry proved totally inadequate against German superior numbers amply supplied with tanks and aircraft. The small Polish air force was soon out of action and Hitler's Stukas unhindered could dive-bomb cities, military transports and refugees alike. Within a fortnight the Germans were at the gates of Warsaw, Marshal Rydz-Smigley's armies beating a hasty, confused, but fighting retreat.

On 15th September Rydz-Smigly realized that the defence of Poland had collapsed. He issued orders for a withdrawal of the bulk of the forces to the south-eastern tip of the country, a wedge between the Soviet Union, Hungary and Rumania. There he hoped to hold a short, defensive line, obtaining his supplies through the allied Rumania. He did not know that the Nazi-Soviet pact of non-agression, signed by Ribbentrop and Molotov on the eve of the invasion, included a secret protocol in which Germany and Russia agreed to partition Poland between them.

On 17th September Russian troops crossed the frontier in strength. Still the Poles refused to surrender. Warsaw withstood another ten days of bombardment, some other towns held out until the beginning of October. The last battle between Polish and German troops ended on 5th October.

Shocked by the swift collapse, stunned by having found themselves once more squashed between the German hammer and the Russian anvil, the Poles still did not capitulate. President Moscicki, his Government, and Marshal Rydz-Smigly all escaped to Rumania where their nominal allies promptly interned them. Prevented from further action the President resigned and, in accordance with the Constitution, transferred his office to the Speaker of the Senate, Ladislas Raczkiewicz, who happened to be in Paris.

Meanwhile in Poland the nightmare of the Nazi reign began. The Germans had occupied the whole of western and central Poland up to the line of the River Bug, leaving the rest to the Russians. Now the German share was divided into two parts: the north-western half and Silesia were incorporated into the Reich, while the remainder, which included Warsaw, became a German colony under the name of 'Government-General' with the capital in Cracow.

Nazi policy in the incorporated provinces was simple. 'It will be my task,' said Gauleiter Forster at Bydgoszcz (27th November 1939), 'to remove every manifestation of Polonism within the next few years. . . .' His colleague Gauleiter Greiser declared in a speech at Gniezno a year later: 'For the first time in German history we are politically exploiting our victories. Not even an inch of the land we have conquered will ever belong to a Pole again. Poles can work for us, but not as rulers, only as serfs.'

In the dispassionate words of a German historian: 'The Polish intelligentsia and all officials, politicians and leaders of Polish associations were eliminated or killed as early as the late autumn of 1939 . . . the Poles were not only subject to special regulations but were also kept far below the German level in conditions of work, pay and rations.'[1] After all Dr. Robert Ley, Hitler's close collaborator and the head of the *Arbeitsfront* formulated the policy quite clearly: 'A lower race needs less space, less nourishment and less culture than a higher race. Never can the Germans live under the same conditions as the Poles and the Jews.'

In the incorporated territories the Poles became slaves, working for the Germans and living at their whim and mercy. According to German estimates one province alone, Wartheland as they called it (with the capital in Poznan), lost during the war 'through murder, resettlement and deportation, some 390,000 Polish and about 380,000 Jewish inhabitants, or in other words one sixth of its 1939 population'.[2] Their place was taken by about a quarter of a million Germans from Russia, from the Baltic states and from other regions. The remaining Poles became a race of helots, men not being allowed to marry under the age of twenty-eight and women under twenty-five, prohibited any access to secondary or university education, treated often worse than cattle.

In the remaining part of German-occupied Poland, in the so called General-Government, the fate of the people was no better, though few serious attempts were made to colonize the country with Germans. Lest the Poles should harbour any illusions, the Governor-General, Dr. Hans Frank, said in a speech at Christmas 1940: 'The Polish State has ceased to exist and will

[1] Prof. Hans Roos: *A History of Modern Poland* translated by J. R. Foster, London, 1966.

[2] Ibid.

never return to life. Let the Poles never forget that they must blame themselves for their fate. They have no historical mission whatever in this part of the world. If they had such a mission, God would have blessed them.' On another occasion Frank said: 'The Poles do not need universities or secondary schools; the Polish lands are to be changed into an intellectual desert.'

If Frank did not entirely succeed, it was not for want of trying. Already at the beginning of November 1939, all the professors of the University and of the Academy of Mines in Cracow received an invitation to a meeting to be held in the great hall of the University on the 6th of that month; a German speaker would address them on 'The attitude of the German Authorities to Science and Teaching'. The professors assembled as requested and discovered that the speaker was Dr. Meyer, the chief of the Gestapo in Cracow. He told them in a few words that since they had been planning to resume their lectures, had not interrupted their scientific work, and since 'the University of Cracow had been a bastion of Polonism for more than five hundred years', they were now all under arrest.

To the accompaniment of kicking and beating, the professors, some of them very old men, were bundled into cars and taken first to prison, later to be sent to German concentration camps, where they were tortured for several months. Many of them never came back. Altogether the German occupation claimed as victims more than four hundred Polish university teachers.

In a systematic campaign to eradicate Polish culture, libraries and art collections, both public and private, were plundered, street names changed, monuments blown up, church treasures removed to Germany. . . . The dismal list is long but the German war against art and culture pales in comparison with the sum of human suffering and degradation inflicted on the whole conquered people: two and a half million people deported as slave labourers, mainly to Germany, a similar number expelled from their homes, with nothing but the clothes they were wearing and the few belonging they could carry, and transported in cattle trucks to unknown destinations.

Cold statistics cannot even begin to illustrate the horror of thousands and millions of men, women and children dying in concentration camps, gassed, killed by firing squads, frozen to death in deportation trains, shot in the streets, tortured to death by the Gestapo. 7,500 doctors, 5,500 judges and lawyers, 16,000 teachers, 2,600 Roman Catholic priests perished.[1] Altogether, out of a population of some 35 million at the outbreak of war, more than six million died as the result of the war, but only one in ten of those was killed as the result of the hostilities. The torture and death chambers of German concentration camps alone claimed more than three and a half million people, among them at least two and a half million Jews.

The Jews, of course, suffered by far the worst fate. For them the Nazis were preparing the 'final solution' and Poland was to be the scene of this genocide. First the Jews were herded in ghettoes, where starvation and disease took their toll at an increasing rate. But this was too slow for the Germans, and mass transports of Jews started leaving the ghettoes for the extermination camps of Auschwitz (Oswiecim) and Treblinka, Majdanek, Belzec and Sobibor.

In Warsaw the daily rate of deportation from the ghetto to Treblinka reached 10,000 by October 1942. Realizing at last the full horror of their position and the true aim of the Nazis, the Jews in the Warsaw ghetto rose in arms on 19th April 1943. Their desperate and hopeless struggle lasted four weeks, with German artillery firing point blank and the Nazis destroying building after building, until only rubble was left of what used to be a large and populous district of the city.

This was the first of two risings in Warsaw during the war. The second came on 1st August 1944, when Warsaw could hear the sound of advancing Soviet guns, and the doom of Nazi Germany was already sealed. The Polish secret Home Army, some 50,000 strong in the capital, managed at first to capture most of the city. But the Soviet advance was halted, the Germans brought up reinforcements and started a systematic reconquest of the city in house to house fighting. Two months after the beginning of the rising, when food, ammunition and medical supplies were completely exhausted, the surviving Poles finally surrendered on 2nd October. Their losses in dead amounted to 16,000 soldiers of the Home Army and more than 150,000 civilians.

As an act of vengeance for the rising Hitler ordered that Warsaw should be razed to the ground. The survivors were

[1] *Poland in Figures*, Warsaw, 1964.

ordered out and German demolition squads moved in. When they finished their work about 85 per cent of all the buildings were completely destroyed. A city of 1,300,000 inhabitants ceased to exist.

These are some of the facts imprinted on the collective memory of the Poles. But each of them has also his own, private memories of friends and relations killed or maimed; many remember vividly being hunted like animals or tortured inside Gestapo prisons and concentration camps, living in 'continual fear and danger of violent death'.

They have not forgotten, they do not want to forget, and they will not let their children forget. The experience of Hitler's Reich, superimposed on the more distant memories reaching as far back as the Teutonic Knights, have made the Poles alert to the slightest sign of revival of German nationalism. On this, if on little else, they are at one with the Russians. They believe that the present division of Germany is in their interest and they would like to make it permanent. A Pole, when asked about the desirability of reuniting Germany is likely to answer: 'God forbid. I'd rather divide them into a dozen states.'

17

THE UNDERGROUND STATE

In October 1939, after they occupied the whole of the country, both Hitler and Stalin thought that they had buried Poland for good. They should have known better. Suddenly the words of their National Anthem, 'Poland is not yet lost as long as we are alive', regained their full, old meaning for the Poles. After only twenty years of independence it was easy for them to revert to their traditional fight for freedom and conspiracy against alien rule. They proceeded to build two parallel state organizations, one acting in the open from Allied soil, the other operating secretly in Poland itself.

Even Polish communists, who can claim credit for taking part in neither, admit nowadays a grudging pride in the war-time achievements of the two states. The exploits of the Polish forces in the West and of the underground army at home, have added another important chapter to the long story of the nation's struggle for independence and this too, colours present-day attitudes.

Though the defeat of September 1939 was complete, though their country was once more partitioned between two mighty states, the Poles never regarded the foreign occupation as anything but temporary and from the very beginning started plotting against the invaders and preparing to resume the open fight.

Abroad the continuity of legal government was preserved when Ignacy Moscicki, prevented from exercising the office of President of the Republic (since he was interned in Rumania), resigned in favour of Ladislas Racekiewicz in Paris. The new President appointed a Government-in-exile under the premiership of General Ladislas Sikorski, a distinguished soldier and former Prime Minister of liberal views and an unblemished record of opposition to the Pilsudski regime. Sikorski's cabinet was a coalition of the four main former opposition parties: the right-wing National Democrats, Sikorski's own small Christian Labour Party, the Peasant Party and the socialist P.P.S. Only the extreme right-wing fascist O.N.R. (the National-Radical Camp which had come into prominence during the last years before the war), the communists (who were an insignificant force), and the numerous but now bewildered and disorganized supporters of the former Pilsudski regime did not participate, though some of the latter soon joined the Sikorski Government.

As a demonstration of their intention to restore parliamentary democracy, the Poles also set up a National Council in Angers, consisting of nineteen politicians representing the four coalition parties and the Jewish national minority. Another former Prime Minister, the famous pianist Paderewski, now in his seventy-ninth year, became its Speaker.

The Western Allies promptly recognized the Sikorski Government, as did most of the neutrals, including the U.S.A., but not the U.S.S.R. With allied help the Sikorski Government turned to its first urgent task: the creation of a Polish Army in the West. Many members of Polish armed forces, having escaped to Latvia, Lithuania, Hungary and Rumania, made their way to France and, together with the numerous Polish emigrants there and volunteers from all over the world, they quickly formed new fighting units. By the spring of 1940 Poland again had an Army of three divisions and one brigade, a total of well over 80,000 men, and a sizeable air force. Another Polish unit, the independent Carpathian Brigade was formed in Syria, while the bulk of the small but efficient Polish Navy, having escaped from the Baltic, was already operating alongside the Royal Navy.

When the Germans invaded Norway the Polish forces abroad went into action—a mountain brigade and two destroyers took part in the ill-fated Narvik expedition. Then came the German invasion in the west, followed by the French collapse and with it also, it seemed at the time, the end of Poland-in-exile. Two Polish infantry divisions were forced to cross into Switzerland, where they were interned. But most of the remaining forces in France, together with the Sikorski Government and the National Council, managed to make their way to Britain. For the next five years London became the capital of Poland.

The Carpathian Brigade, still intact, was transferred from

Syria to Palestine, later to fight with distinction at Tobruk, while the forces in Britain were reformed and provided with new arms. The Air Force, which eventually grew to ten fighter and four bomber squadrons, played an important part in the Battle of Britain and subsequent operations, while the army was being trained for the invasion of France.

After the German attack on Russia in 1941, Sikorski concluded an agreement with Stalin which provided for the formation of a Polish Army in the U.S.S.R. In the spring and summer of 1942 these units, under the command of General Anders, were evacuated from the Soviet Union via Persia to the Middle Eastern theatre. Together with the Carpathian Brigade they formed the 2nd Polish Corps, which fought in the Italian campaign, taking Monte Cassino by storm and liberating Ancona and Bologna. At the same time a Polish armoured division from Britain was fighting in Normandy at Falaise, later helping in the liberation of northern France, Belgium and Holland, while the Polish parachute brigade took part in the Battle of Arnhem.

By the end of the war, in spite of heavy losses suffered in so many battles, the Polish forces in the West numbered well over two hundred thousand men. Not unreasonably they felt that they were good allies who had contributed their share to the Western war effort. All the more bitter was their disappointment and anger at the tragic fate of their comrades of the underground army in Poland and the fate of the country itself.

There is something of a Greek tragedy in the story of the underground state and army in Poland. How that vast organization was created at the height of the Gestapo terror, while S.S. detachments roamed the streets, rounding up people for forced labour or summary execution, is one of the great sagas of the Second World War; how the Polish resistance movement fought on the winning side and yet lost all, is one of the grimmest chapters of recent history.

The first recorded secret organization was set up in Warsaw even before the September campaign came to an end. On 27th September 1939, while the city was still defending itself, a number of army officers met in Warsaw and agreed to form an underground organization to continue the struggle under German occupation. They gave it the name of 'Service for

Polish Victory' (S.Z.P.). General Tokarzewski became its Commander and Colonel Rowecki the Chief of Staff. This purely military nucleus soon acquired a political character when, in November 1939, the Central Council of S.Z.P. was set up with the participation of leading politicians from the three biggest parties of the Sikorski coalition: the National Democrats, the Peasant Party and the P.P.S. The direction of S.Z.P. established contact with the Government-in-exile and tried to consolidate the resistance movement at home.

The need for consolidation was acute. Already early in 1940 there were at least one hundred separate underground organizations in existence. Some of them, born out of the initiative of patriotic individuals, had only few members, others, organized by the various political parties, counted them in thousands. All shades of political opinion were detectable in this underground movement, with the sole exception of the communists who, bewildered by the Soviet-German co-operation, lacking any direction or organizational framework, just watched developments in hopeless confusion until Hitler decided to invade Russia.

The task of consolidating the underground movement was not easy. Mutual suspicion between the various political parties and splinter groups, between those who had stayed behind in Poland and those who had gone into exile, rivalry between organizations with similar aims, and the personal ambitions of many of the leaders all contributed to the difficulties. To complicate matters still further, many of the large political organizations had their own armed detachments and were none too keen to incorporate them into a unified fighting force. But by a process of patient negotiations between the various groupings in Poland and between them and the Government in London, the unification of the bulk of the underground was achieved.

By the beginning of 1942 most of the secret fighting formations were amalgamated into one single Home Army (A.K.) under the command of Colonel Rowecki, who was raised by Sikorski to the rank of General. The Government-in-exile was represented in Poland by a Minister Plenipotentiary, responsible for political liaison with the A.K., with London and with the leadership of the main parties in Poland. Under the Minister

Plenipotentiary a vast underground administrative network was set up. Secret Polish courts tried the most vicious of German war criminals and special armed detachments were responsible for executing the verdicts of these courts. In one month alone, May 1953, one of the underground newspapers carried notices of the passing and execution of fifty death sentences on members of the Gestapo.

The Polish underground press helped to keep the nation informed during the dark days under occupation. Well over a hundred different publications, some of them ephemeral, others appearing regularly each week, reached the public and were widely read in spite of the death penalty threatening anyone found in possession of one of those illegal sheets. Apart from reprinting the news monitored from London, and disseminating announcements from the underground authorities, the resistance press also engaged in a vigorous re-thinking of Polish policies and attitudes for the future. Since the Germans had closed all universities and secondary schools, the Poles also organized a network of clandestine schools to continue the education of the young. They even had two underground universities.

During the earlier stages of the war the underground state and army set themselves a number of limited objectives to sustain the morale of the nation by information, exhortation and counter terrorism, to hamper the German war effort by sabotage and passive resistance, to help the Allies by supplying information about German troop movements and other developments of military significance (the Polish underground was the first to alert London about the development of the V weapons) and to prepare for the final armed struggle. Open warfare against the Germans was ruled out, except in special local circumstances, until such time there was a chance of ultimate success, instead of just inviting still more savage German reprisals. This was a sensible realistic policy, fully endorsed both by the Sikorski Government and by the Western Allies, but it brought on the A.K. and the whole underground movement the wrath of the communists.

The communists themselves did not become active in Poland on any scale until after the German invasion of Russia, but now they were itching for action. They accused the A.K. of being anti-Soviet, which was true in so far as the A.K. in common with the great majority of the nation was anti-communist and would not recognize that Russia had any right to Poland's eastern territories. On the other hand the A.K. had clear instructions to co-operate with the approaching Soviet armies and did so with disastrous results which are described in the next chapter. The communists also claimed that the A.K. has strong fascist leanings and was inclined to co-operate with the Germans. There is little evidence to support either charge, except in relation to a different underground organization, the N.S.Z., created by extreme right-wing elements, which operated independently of the A.K. and did engage in denouncing and fighting both Jews and Communists. Only in April 1944, after the N.S.Z. had split up into two wings, did the more moderate wing of the N.S.Z. join the A.K.

What of the communists themselves? They, too, formed their own fighting detachments, which showed conspicuous courage, but their strength was never great even after amalgamation with several other extreme left-wing units. According to their own estimates the 'Peoples' Army' (A.L.), which was the result of a merger of communist and other extreme left-wing detachments, numbered only 60,000.[1] By contrast, the A.K. under General Bor-Komorowski, who succeeded General Rowecki after the latter's arrest by the Germans, numbered in the years 1943–44 at least 300,000 men and some sources put its strength as high as 380,000.

There was little or no co-operation between the two underground fighting forces, but on one memorable occasion they did join hands. This happened during the Warsaw rising in 1944, which started on Bor-Komorowski's orders when the Soviet forces were at the gates of the capital. Possibly because they believed communist propaganda put out by Soviet-controlled radio stations which were calling the people to rise in arms, or because they had been out of touch with their political masters, the communist A.L. detachments in Warsaw joined the A.K. in the insurrection. Both fought bravely and with fantastic tenacity, but in vain, for it was Stalin's wish that the Polish underground movement be destroyed and the country turned into an obedient Soviet satellite.

[1] Jerzy Pawlowicz: *Z Najnowszych Dziejow Polski*, Warsaw, 1963.

18

STALIN AND THE POLES

Scratch a Russian communist and you will find a Russian chauvinist.

V. Lenin at the 8th Congress of the Soviet Communist Party

The record of Stalin's policy towards Poland is a textbook case of utterly ruthless conquest. Already in 1920 his purpose was plain; in a letter to Lenin dated 20th June he wrote about 'Soviet Germany, Soviet Poland, Soviet Hungary and Soviet Finland'. Two months later Pilsudski's victory in the Battle of Warsaw barred the Russian advance into central Europe. But Stalin was not a man to give up. He waited patiently for nineteen years until Hitler presented him with an opening.

In the summer of 1939 an Anglo-French mission was in Moscow trying to find out on what terms the Soviet Union would join the Allies if Hitler attacked Poland. Stalin made the entry of Soviet troops into Poland into a condition of aid. The Poles, with their long memories of Russian occupation, the Soviet march on Warsaw in 1920, and the claims to her eastern territories made by Russia on behalf of the Ukrainians and Byelorussians, not unnaturally refused. Still the Moscow talks dragged on, with the Western Allies unaware that Stalin was simultaneously negotiating with Berlin, until the unexpected announcement on 23rd August 1939 of the German-Soviet pact of non-aggression which gave Hitler the green light for his invasion of Poland. But the full meaning of that pact did not become obvious until the early hours of 17th September.

On that day, the Soviet Government peremptorily informed the Poles (with whom it still had a valid treaty of non-aggression) that the Polish State had ceased to exist and they were sending forces 'to protect the Byelorussian and Ukrainian population'. Twelve days later Molotov and Ribbentrop signed a treaty of partition, by which the Soviet Union annexed just over half of the territory of the Polish Republic (over 77,000 square miles out of a total of 150,000 square miles), Hitler retaining the rest. The frontier followed roughly the so called 'Curzon line', giving the Soviet Union the cities of Lvov and Vilno and a Polish population of about five million (this according to the last Polish census; the Russians estimated the number of Poles at only about three million) out of a total of thirteen million.

In an apparently magnanimous gesture Stalin decided to give the Vilno district to the Lithuanian Republic, knowing full well that his next step was the incorporation into the Soviet Union of the whole of that country together with the other two Baltic states. In the remainder of eastern Poland elections were held for West Byelorussian and West Ukrainian 'Peoples' Assemblies'. Conducted on the well-known Soviet pattern these elections produced no surprises; the candidates on the single lists obtained over 90 per cent of the votes and the two Assemblies duly voted for incorporation into the Soviet Union.

Already before the elections the Soviet secret police had moved in and prisons were overflowing with Poles, including a number of communists. In the city of Lvov alone the rate of arrests reached the figure of five hundred a day. Soon systematic deportations of Poles also started, gradually gathering momentum and assuming mass proportions during 1940. Altogether at least one and a half million Poles were deported to 'forced settlement' or labour camps in the northern, central and eastern Soviet Union. The inhuman conditions of those deportations differed little from what the Germans were doing in the rest of the country, but the vastness in the Soviet Union meant journeys lasting weeks rather than days in packed and unheated railway waggons, often through the depth of the Russian winter. There were no mass executions and no indiscriminate shooting of innocent people, but the callous inhumanity of the operation claimed thousands of victims. About a third of the deported Poles—half a million people—were sent to forced labour camps, where excessive work combined with a starvation diet killed a quarter of them.

All these facts came to light after Hitler's attack on Russia, which forced Stalin to a temporary and more apparent than real change in his Polish policy. From the British point of view it was clearly intolerable that two of the allies, Poland and the Soviet Union, should be in a state of undeclared war with each other, and the Foreign Office set to work for reconciliation. On 30th July 1941 a Polish-Soviet agreement was concluded. It declared the German-Soviet treaty of partition null and void, provided for a resumption of diplomatic relations between the Sikorski Government and the Soviet Union, and mutual help in the war against Germany.

What the new agreement did not say specifically, though this was implied in the statement that the treaty of partition had become void, was that the Polish-Soviet frontier remained where it had been on 1st September 1939. This omission caused a storm among exiled Poles and led to the resignation of three ministers from the Sikorski Government. Sikorski however, was determined to operate the agreement loyally, even though Stalin's true intentions soon became clear. Not only did he drop more or less veiled hints at frontier revision (these Sikorski refused to discuss) but he would not allow Ukrainians, Byelorussians and Jews, who were Polish citizens, to join the Polish army which General Anders now started to organize in the Soviet Union. Two leaders of the Jewish socialist party *Bund*, Victor Alter and Henryk Erlich, who wanted to form separate Jewish units in the Polish army, were shot on Stalin's orders as traitors.

Still, there was no shortage of men wishing to join the army. One of the results of the Polish-Soviet agreement was 'an amnesty' for all Poles deported into the Soviet Union, and tens of thousands of them, ill, starved and in rags, were flocking to Polish recruiting centres. Stalin, having first set an upper limit on the strength of the Polish army, demanded impatiently that each small unit, as soon as it was organized, should be sent to the front. The Poles objected. Their soldiers were still in a poor physical condition and the Russians had not even made sufficient food available. Also the Polish authorities did not wish to see their new and still unready army destroyed piecemeal in the savage fighting on the eastern front. Stalin retaliated by reducing the maximum size of the army from 96,000 to 44,000, while already more than 70,000 had enrolled in it. At this stage the Poles decided to evacuate the army to Persia.

The grudging, hostile alliance between Stalin and Sikorski lasted nearly two years, as long as the military situation of the Soviet Union remained critical. Early in 1943, when the victory at Stalingrad turned the tide in his favour, Stalin became explicit. In a note of 2nd March the Soviet Government rejected Polish claims to the eastern part of the country. Since the Poles remained adamant, Stalin decided to break with the Sikorski Government. All he now needed was a pretext.

In April 1943 the Germans announced the discovery of graves of thousands of Polish Army Officers in the forest of Katyn, near Smolensk and accused the Russians of the mass murder. The Sikorski Government, which had tried in vain to discover from the Russians what had happened to more than seven thousand officers taken prisoner by the Red Army in 1939, now suggested that the matter should be investigated by the International Red Cross. Stalin replied by breaking off diplomatic relations with the Poles.

His indignation at the 'unfriendly act' of the Polish Government sounds somewhat hollow, since the Russians never succeeded in shifting on to the Germans the responsibility for the Katyn mass murders and failed to produce any convincing evidence of German guilt for this particular crime during the Nuremberg trials.

In the midst of the Katyn crisis Sikorski was killed in an air crash at Gibraltar and the leader of the Peasant Party, Stanislas Mikolajczyk, took over the Premiership of the Government-in-exile. He made repeated attempts to heal the breach with the Russians but achieved nothing. Stalin was determined to deal only with a subservient Polish administration and he already had a nucleus of it available in the shape of the 'League of Polish Patriots', a small communist organization in the U.S.S.R. The next step was the formation in Russia of a communist-led Polish division, which was given the patriotic sounding name of Kosciuszko, after the hero of the first Polish insurrection against the Russians! Then followed the transformation of the communist 'League of Polish Patriots' into a more respectable-looking, but still communist-dominated 'Committee of National Liberation', which the Russians treated as if it were the legitimate government of Poland.

As the Soviet armies crossed the 1939 frontier the A.K., in obedience to the orders it had received from the Polish Government in London, went into action against the Germans and substantially helped the Soviet advance. But as soon as the

Germans were out of sight, the Russians interned the A.K. Detachments, usually arresting all the Polish officers. By the summer of 1944 the Russians were approaching Warsaw and the 'Committee of National Liberation' was already installed in Lublin as a provision government of the liberated territories west of the Ribbentrop-Molotov line. Soviet radio stations broadcast repeated appeals to the people of Warsaw to rise against the Germans. On 29th July, for instance, the following Soviet broadcast in Polish was monitored in London:

> No doubt Warsaw already hears the guns of the battle, which is going to bring her liberation. Those who have never bowed their heads to the Hitlerite power will again, as in 1939, join battle with the Germans, this time for decisive action. . . . Poles, the time of liberation is at hand. Poles, to arms! There is not a moment to lose!

In spite of the depressing reports he had received from eastern Poland about the treatment of the Home Army by the Russians, the Commander-in-Chief of the A.K. decided to strike in the capital. On 1st August the A.K. seized key points in the city and the Warsaw rising began.

Mikolajczyk was in Moscow at the time, negotiating about the formation of a new Polish coalition government. He saw Stalin on 3rd August and asked for immediate help for Warsaw, especially tanks, artillery and ammunition. Stalin at first denied that any fighting was taking place in the Polish capital, but promised to look into the matter. A few days later Mikolajczyk again saw Stalin and this time obtained a promise of help. But instead of helping Warsaw, the Russian advance halted in the eastern suburbs of the capital. From across the Vistula the Red Army watched the Poles fight their desperate battle.

To make quite sure of the outcome Stalin refused Allied requests to allow British and American planes to refuel on Soviet airfields after dropping supplies for Warsaw. Several personal appeals from Churchill and Roosevelt failed to make any impression on him. In one of his replies to the Western leaders he used a significant sentence: 'Sooner or later the truth about the group of criminals who have embarked on the Warsaw adventure in order to seize power will become known to everybody.'

From that moment onwards there was no room for doubt—the Poles would not be allowed to 'seize power' in their own country. That was why Stalin condemned the Home Army to death. Without firing a shot he was the real victor in the Battle of Warsaw.

But the A.K. outside Warsaw and the organization of the underground state still existed and had to be eliminated. In March, 1945, when the capital was in Russian hands, the most prominent leaders of the Polish underground, including the new C.-in-C. of the A.K. and the Minister Plenipotentiary, were enticed to Warsaw with the promise of a safe conduct to negotiate with the Russians. They were promptly arrested and tried by a Russian court in Moscow, fifteen of them receiving sentences of long-term imprisonment.

The rest was easy. Within a few months Stalin's armies were in possession of the whole of Poland and he could dictate his terms. At Yalta the Western Allies agreed to the Soviet demand for a revision of the Polish-Soviet frontier in accordance with Stalin's wishes. For most Poles this was a bitter blow, for it meant giving up two great Polish cities, Vilno and Lvov, which for many centuries had been centres of Polish culture. It also meant surrendering to the Soviet Union about half of pre-war Poland with several million Polish inhabitants. The Poles wanted compensation for these losses. At Potsdam Stalin gave it to them at the expense of Germany.

East Prussia, the former seat of the Teutonic Knights and the cradle of Prussian militarism, disappeared from the map, divided between Russia and Poland, while in the west Stalin pushed the Polish frontier to the rivers Oder and Neisse. He gave to the Poles territories which had not been theirs since the days of Mieszko and Boleslas the Brave, inhabited by about seven million Germans with only a small sprinkling of people of Polish origin. In this way he made sure that in the future the establishment of friendly Polish-German relations would be more difficult than ever, and Poland would always have to rely on Soviet support.

The Western Allies agreed at Potsdam to the new Polish-German frontier only as a temporary administrative arrangement, subject to ratification by the German peace conferance. They also insisted at Yalta that the Soviet-sponsored Provisional

Government of Poland, before it could be recognized had to acquire a representative and democratic character and undertake to hold free elections.

Stalin agreed to these demands, knowing that he was in full control of the situation. Mikolajczyk, who had resigned the Premiership of the Government-in-exile together with three other non-communists, decided to join the Provisional Government of National Unity now firmly established in Warsaw. He

became Vice-Premier and Minister of Agriculture, but all the key posts, including the all important one of Minister of Public Security, remained firmly in the hands of Stalin's nominees. This, however, was sufficient for the Western Allies to recognize the Warsaw Government, and to withdraw recognition from the Government-in-exile.

In January 1947 the first general election took place in Poland. According to the Yalta agreement it was to have been 'free and unfettered', but such an election would have produced an overwhelming vote against the communists. Stalin's henchmen made sure of the result by a combination of terror and fraud. Mikolajczyk's Polish Peasant Party, which in any free election would have won the greatest share of seats, was reduced to twenty-eight deputies in the Seym composed of 444.

The way was now clear for a complete Sovietization of Poland. All the opponents of the regime were eliminated, forced to flee abroad, like Mikolajczyk, browbeaten into compliance, or imprisoned. Step by step Poland was turned into a perfect satellite state, obedient to the orders of Moscow, ruled by the all-powerful secret police, exploited by the Soviet Union like few colonies have ever been exploited. Stalin had realized his old aim of a Soviet Poland and much else besides. His empire had become vaster than the Tsar's.

In the process of achieving his total victory over Poland, while he was at war with Germany, Stalin demolished the proud independence of the Polish State, forcibly shifted the whole country westward, while imposing on it the hateful communist regime from the east. His actions re-opened the old wounds dating back to the century of Tsarist oppression, and inflicted new ones. As if wanting to make sure that these wounds would not heal, the despot of the communist world added insult to injury; he appointed as Poland's Minister of Defence the Soviet Marshal, Constantin Rokossovsky, a man of Polish origin, best known as the commander of the Soviet Army who did not come to the aid of Warsaw during the rising, and stood by watching the city die.

PART FIVE

HALF-FREEDOM, HALF-INDEPENDENCE

Catholic Poland. The Monastery at Czestochowa, the focal point of the cult of Virgin Mary, attracts millions of pilgrims. The Primate, Cardinal Wyszynski, is an outspoken critic of communism

Nuns in the Old City square in Warsaw. Completely destroyed by the Germans in 1944, the square has been lovingly rebuilt stone by stone

19

STALINISM IN POLAND

> The Polish People's Republic is a country of people's democracy, based on the alliance between workers and peasants.
>
> The Polish Popular Encyclopaedia

'People's democracy' is a euphemism for a communist-ruled country. Yet, Poland has no communist party, or at least there is no party of such name and there has not been one since 1938. This apparent paradox illustrates some of the problems of Polish communism and its difficult relations both with Moscow and with the Polish people.

Yet, the Polish communist movement has a long tradition, dating back to the last century, and the S.D.K.P., was among the first communist parties in the world. What then went wrong with Polish communism? Primarily two things, and both grew in importance as time passed. The first was the conflict between communism and the Polish will for national independence, the second was the ideological divergence between Polish communists and Stalin himself.

Partly under the influence of Rosa Luxemburg, the S.D.K.P. was entirely internationalist in outlook and opposed the Polish struggle for independence, preferring to work for international revolution instead. This immediately removed any appeal communism could have made to the minds of the overwhelming majority of patriotically inclined Poles who, if they had left-wing views, found the P.P.S., which stood for independence, much more attractive. When the First World War ended and Poland became a state once more, the communists regarded the new Republic as an ephemeral, semi-feudal creation and chose to remain an illegal party.

At that time the S.D.K.P. i L. (as it was called by then) amalgamated with the left wing of the P.P.S. and formally adopted the name of the Communist Party of Polish Workers

(K.P.R.P.). Had they decided to come out into the open, the party would certainly have been dissolved by the Warsaw authorities during the Polish-Soviet war.

When the war reached its climax and the Red Army was marching on Warsaw, Lenin expected both a swift conquest and a revolution in Poland. In his impatience he set up in the town of Bialystok a Polish Revolutionary Committee composed of communists who had lived abroad for many years, with the dreaded Dzerzhinsky of the *Cheka* as one of its members. But Pilsudski won the Battle of Warsaw, there was no revolution in Poland and in the popular mind Polish communists became permanently identified with allegiance to Moscow. The change of name of the party to the Communist Party of Poland (K.P.P.) in 1925, which implied at least a recognition of the state, did not help matters much and by that time the K.P.P. was already seriously embroiled with Stalin.

In Stalin's eyes the Polish party suffered from the fatal deviation called 'Luxemburgism' and later committed the unpardonable crime of showing support for Trotsky, As early as 1924 the Comintern dismissed the entire Central Committee of the Polish party, appointing a new one instead. A year later this new Committee was also dismissed in a body. Stalin never trusted the K.P.P. and eventually destroyed it. The exact details of what happened are still uncertain, but this much is known:

In 1937 on Stalin's orders many thousands of Polish communists, who were either living in the Soviet Union, or happened to be there on party business, or had come in answer to a special summons, were suddenly arrested. Almost the entire leadership of the K.P.P. and also the leaders of the Polish communist brigade fighting in Spain were among the victims. It is not known precisely how many people were arrested and how many of those were executed, but according to Polish communist sources the number of those who lost their lives amounted to several thousand.[1] The toll among the leaders was particularly heavy: of the twenty-one leading personalities of the K.P.P. who were alive at the beginning of 1937 only four survived till the outbreak of the Second World War. Finally,

[1] Richard Hiscocks: *Poland—Bridge for the Abyss?*, Oxford University Press, London, 1963.

some time in 1938 on Stalin's orders the K.P.P. itself was dissolved.

In this way the 1939 war found Polish communists practically without leaders (except for those few who had survived the purge in the security of Polish prisons), without a party and, after the Stalin-Hitler deal, also without a policy. Only after the German invasion of Russia did Stalin discover that he needed a Polish communist party once more. He set up in Moscow a group of little-known Polish communists as an 'Initiative Group' with the task of resurrecting the party. In spite of the fact that Russia was now fighting on the same side as the Poles, conditions were most unfavourable. In the words of a communist writer, there had been 'an increase in anti-Soviet sentiments among the Polish population . . . a decline and partial political isolation of Polish communists'.[1] The 'Initiative Group' decided to play safe in choosing the name of the new party and avoided the term 'communist' altogether. They called it the Polish Workers' Party (P.P.R.) and gave it a respectably patriotic-sounding and politically moderate programme.

During the night of 27th–28th December 1941 six members of the 'Initiative Group' were flown from Moscow in a Soviet plane and landed by parachute near Warsaw. A few days later the inaugural meeting of the P.P.R. took place in a private flat in a Warsaw suburb. Its first secretary-general was Marceli Nowotko, one of the men parachuted into Poland by the Russians. He was shot by an unknown assassin in November 1942 and succeeded in the party post by Paul Finder, another member of the Moscow 'Initiative Group'. But Finder was caught by the Gestapo a year later and another secretary-general had to be appointed. Normally the choice would have been made by Stalin, who undoubtedly would have given the job to another Moscow-trained communist—the P.P.R. being required to rubber-stamp the appointment of their new leader. This time, however, communications between the P.P.R. and Moscow had broken down and thus by pure chance the leadership of the party was free to make its own choice. This fell on Ladislas Gomulka, a home-grown Polish communist who, as far as is known, had never undergone political training in Moscow. Thus the key post in the P.P.R. fell into the hands of a

[1] M. Malinowski: *Z Najnowszych Dziejow Polski*, Warsaw, 1963.

man with an independent mind, whom Stalin neither knew nor trusted. By the time communications with Moscow were restored it was too late to do anything about Gomulka's appointment, since he was greatly respected by the rank and file of the party.

Ladislas Gomulka was born in 1905 near the small town of Krosno in central Galicia. His father worked in an oil refinery and Ladislas at the age of fourteen followed in his footsteps. Soon he became active in the Trade Union movement and joined the P.P.S., but a few years later, after Pilsudski's *coup d'état*, switched his allegiance to the K.P.P. He was only twenty-two but already a veteran of the left-wing movement. Now he rose to the post of secretary of the Chemical Workers' Union, becoming known as a tireless agitator and strike organizer, while showing little interest in the doctrinal struggles within the K.P.P. Neither would he get involved in his party's disagreements with Moscow.

In 1932, while trying to escape arrest, he was shot in the leg by a Polish policeman, captured and sentenced to four years in prison. Released after serving only half his sentence, he returned to his revolutionary activities, only to be arrested again in 1936 and sent to prison, this time for seven years. In the security of that prison Gomulka heard what Stalin had done to his party and to his political friends.

Released on the outbreak of the war, he made his way to Soviet-occupied Lvov. It is reported that with several of his associates he wrote from there to Moscow, asking for permission to join the resistance movement against the Germans—an unwise move to make at a time when Stalin was still on friendly terms with Hitler. When the German attack on Russia came in 1941, Gomulka, instead of escaping to the Soviet Union, deliberately stayed behind until the Germans occupied Lvov and is said to have organized his own partisan group.

A few months after the formation of the P.P.R. he arrived in the capital, joined the party and soon became the secretary of the Warsaw organization and also a member of the Central Committee. In this capacity he launched a violent campaign of terrorism against the Germans in Warsaw, while making attempts to join hands with the A.K. However, since at that time the Katyn massacre became known and Stalin broke off relations with the Polish Government-in-exile, Gomulka's attempt to establish co-operation with the Home Army came at the worst possible psychological moment and it is not surprising that it came to nothing.

After Finder's arrest in the autumn of 1943 came Gomulka's election to the leadership of the P.P.R. An ironic situation. The party, created by Stalin as a tool of his conquest of Poland, found itself led by a genuine patriot, who owed nothing to the Moscow dictator and had not forgotten what Stalin had done to his friends during the great purge. Could Gomulka co-operate with Stalin? Would Stalin co-operate with Gomulka?

Circumstances forced them to do so. Gomulka had no choice at all, short of abandoning his communist creed, and this apparently he would not even consider. Stalin had not much choice either, for he knew that the resurrected Polish communist party was a very tender plant, most unlikely to survive another purge. The long-term aims of the two men were basically different, but they overlapped on one essential point: they both wanted to establish a communist Poland. However, while Stalin wanted to create an obedient satellite, which would mirror conditions in the Soviet Union, Gomulka wanted to develop a Polish brand of communism in a genuinely independent country, though in alliance with the Soviet Union.

There was another point on which both men seemed to be in agreement: the P.P.R. was much too weak to be able to rule Poland alone with any semblance of popular support—it needed as many allies as it could secure. In these circumstances Stalin allowed Gomulka to continue leading the P.P.R. as its secretary-general, while he himself was to rule Poland through trusted, Moscow-trained communists. Chief among them was Boleslas Bierut, an old Comintern agent, who became the first President of the resurrected Polish Republic; Hilary Minc, its economic dictator, and Jacob Berman, the real *eminence grise* of the regime, whose chief lieutenant was the Minister of Public Security, Stanislas Radkiewicz.

As the Red Army pushed the Germans out of Poland and advanced on Berlin, it nominally handed over the administration of the country to the Provisional Government set up by Stalin with real or crypto-communists and some other left-wing elements. The country, ravaged by the war, was the scene of a veritable migration of peoples. Millions of Germans fleeing from Poland's new 'Regained Territories' or expelled from them, millions of Poles drifting away from the eastern provinces incorporated into the Soviet Union, and in addition millions of refugees, deportees, prisoners of war and inmates of concentration camps returning home, often to find the home either destroyed or on the wrong side of the new frontier. Russian troops were everywhere, proclaiming to be friends, but behaving likc an army of occupation.

The nation was tired, hungry, exhausted by more than five years of war and occupation, still suffering from the tragic shock of the Warsaw rising. And against this background of physical and psychological chaos there was only one ray of hope: A Government of National Unity had been set up in Warsaw and it included some members of the former Government-in-exile in London.

Was this the beginning of the end of internal strife?

On closer examination, however, the Government of National Unity neither represented national unity, nor was it united itself. Nominally it was a coalition of at least six parties: the communist P.P.R., the moderate socialist P.P.S., the centre-left Polish Peasant Party (P.S.L.), the communist-dominated Peasant Party (S.L.) and two small centre parties.

The right wing of the political spectrum, which used to be so influential before the war, was not represented at all. The fascist extreme right-wing O.N.R., the more moderate National Democrats, the supporters of the Pilsudski regime and also the Home Army—a large part of the nation—were all condemned as fascists. True, there was an amnesty in 1945 for members of the underground forces who came into the open and surrendered their weapons, but such was the political climate and the mistrust of the communists that only a few thousand men availed themselves of this opportunity. Many more took to the hills and the forests, waging a hopeless but prolonged guerilla war against the communist security forces.

Within the Government of National Unity only two parties were flying their true colours and their representatives really represented their rank and file. There was no doubt that the P.P.R. members of the Government, with Gomulka as Deputy Premier and Minister for the Regained Territories, spoke for their party. Nor could anyone question the fact that Mikolajczyk, another Deputy Premier, who had come from London, enjoyed the support not only of the peasants, but also of a large part of the anti-communist population. As for the rest, the situation was, to say the least, confusing. The Prime Minister, for instance, Edward Osobka-Morawski, was claimed to represent the P.P.S., but if so, which P.P.S., for there seemed to be at least two, one of them faithful to its old democratic programme, the other distinctly pro-communist. The same questions could be raised about other members of the Government, because the old parties had split up and multiplied, borrowing the names of their rivals, until few ordinary people could be sure who stood for what. This, of course, was precisely what the communists wanted to achieve by creating splinter groups of all the parties of the left and the centre.

One fact, however, could not be disguised and confused—Mikolajczyk was anti-communist and he was, probably unwisely, challenging the communists and their allies at the forthcoming elections. When the communists suggested to him an electoral alliance, he demanded 75 per cent of all the parliamentary seats. It is highly probable that in a really free and unfettered election Mikolajczyk would have won a majority of that order, but both Stalin and the Polish communists, Gomulka among them, were determined not to allow it. They had seen the danger sign when the membership of the P.P.R. dropped from about 300,000 in the spring of 1945 to only 160,000 in the summer of that year, while Mikolajczyk's P.S.L. was going from strength to strength and by the end of the year numbered 600,000.

Mikolajczyk placed his faith in the international undertaking that the elections would be free (this had been the condition of the recognition of the Government of National Unity by the Western Allies) and he underestimated the ruthlessness of the communist control of the whole state apparatus. When it came to the voting in January 1947, a combination of terror, trickery and outright falsification reduced the P.S.L. poll to about 10 per cent of the total. British and American protests and P.S.L. objections fell on deaf ears. P.S.L. was out of the Government, and before the end of the year Mikolajczyk was out of the country, forced to flee to the West.

Having thus broken the only serious opposition party, the communists could proceed with the complete Sovietization of Poland. Gomulka had played a leading part in the campaign against Mikolajczyk. It is also known that he was in favour of a merger of the P.P.R. with the P.P.S. (into the Polish United Workers' Party—P.Z.P.R.) and of the P.S.L. with the pro-communist S.L. (forming the United Peasant Party—Z.S.L.) both of which took place within a year or two of the elections. On the other hand there is evidence that he disapproved of the terror of the Security Police and tried to pursue a Polish 'road to socialism', refusing for instance to introduce a forced collectivization of agriculture.

This was held against him when he came into open conflict with Stalin and the Moscow group of Polish communists in 1948. The immediate cause of the breach was Gomulka's opposition to the creation of the Cominform and Stalin's moves against Tito. In Stalin's eyes Gomulka had served his purpose by helping to establish a communist government and liquidate the opposition. Now it was his turn to be liquidated.

It happened almost gently, stage by stage, with the climax coming during a four-day meeting of the Central Committee of the P.P.R. (31st August–3rd September 1948) when Gomulka was accused of nationalist deviation and other crimes in the Stalinist criminal code. The meeting was secret, but it is known that Gomulka, who had been under attack for some time, found himself deserted by his friends and completely isolated. He is said to have made a speech admitting some of the accusations, but justifying his behaviour by the conditions prevailing in Poland. He was removed from the post of secretary-general. A few months later he was deprived of his ministerial posts and after a further interval he and two of his closest collaborators were expelled from the Central Committee of the party. Finally on 31st July 1951 he was arrested.

Meanwhile the full rigours of the Stalinist regime made themselves felt in Poland. Foreign broadcasts were jammed, while press censorship and 'security' legislation reached unprecedented intensity; the Roman Catholic Church found itself under constant attack, with the Primate, Cardinal Wyszynski arrested; peasants were forcibly driven into collectives, the secret police terror was at its worst. And Marshal Rokossovsky became not only Poland's Minister of Defence, but also a member of the Politbureau of the P.Z.P.R.

Later a leading communist was to describe that period in the following words:

> . . . people who were caught in the streets and released after seven days of interrogation, unfit to live. These people had to be taken to lunatic asylums. Others sought refuge in the asylums to avoid the security police. Men in panic, even honest men, were fleeing abroad to escape our system. . . . The whole city knew that people were being murdered, the whole city knew that there were cells in which people were kept for three weeks standing in excrements . . . cold water was poured on people who were left in the cold to freeze. . . .[1]

In other words, after Gomulka's fall, Poland was going through the same Stalinist nightmare which hung over a large part of Europe. But there was just one difference which was to become important later: unlike other 'deviationists' in the other satellite countries, Gomulka was not executed. He lived to see another day.

[1] Leon Wudzki in a speech to the Central Committee of the P.Z.P.R. on 20th October 1956.

20

SPRING IN OCTOBER

> This is spring in October, the spring of awakened hopes and awakened national pride, the spring of true international proletarianism and of determined will to mark out our own Polish way to socialism.
>
> Henry Holland on Warsaw Radio,
> 21st October 1956

In October 1956, like so many times before, Poland was on the brink of an uprising. There had been workers' riots in Poznan earlier in the year, and now the whole country was boiling with discontent, voicing its protest, demanding change. The air in Warsaw was thick with rumours of plots and intrigues, of sinister Russian troop movements and Polish counter-moves; workers and students were holding mass meetings and passing spontaneous resolutions, the intellectuals were in open revolt. Like in November 1830 it only needed a spark to produce a violent explosion.

The sudden and completely unexpected arrival in Warsaw of Krushchev, accompanied by three Soviet Deputy Premiers and a posse of Russian officers, on the morning of 19th October nearly produced that fatal spark, nearly but not quite. For in the event there was no uprising in Poland and no violent revolution. Yet a fundamental upheaval did take place, changing profoundly not only the nature of the communist regime, but also Poland's relations with the Soviet Union, and all this without a shot being fired.

Were the Poles acting out of character, forgetting their reckless and heroic past, or were the circumstances entirely without precedent? The answer is—both. The Poles, with the Warsaw rising of 1944 still fresh in their memories, had learnt some bitter lessons, and both the internal and international situation of the country was extremely complex, with conflicting forces often operating in the same direction.

Superficially the conditions in Poland resembled to a certain extent those in the Congress Kingdom in 1830, when the November rising against Tsarist rule erupted in the streets of Warsaw. Then as now a Russian was in command of the Polish Army, then as now the popular demand was for independence from Russia. But here the similarity ends. Marshal Rokossovsky was not another Grand Duke Constantine, and Nikita Kruschev, in spite of all his ruthlessness and dictatorial tendencies, would have been ill-cast in the role of Nicholas I. More important still, there were no Russian troops in Germany and in Poland in 1830, and there was no equivalent to the P.Z.P.R., with its all-pervading influence, which could change direction, nor was there a Gomulka waiting in the wings to effect the necessary changes.

The 'revolutionary' demands had been formulated on behalf of the whole country by the workers of Poznan, when they went on strike and then took to the streets in June 1956. They carried banners and posters with slogans like these:

> We want bread!
> Lower prices—increase wages!
> Down with the Russians!
> We want freedom!
> Down with false communism!
> Down with dictatorship!
> Down with the Soviet occupation!

After the police had fraternized with the strikers and some army units refused to take action against them, the Government succeeded in suppressing the Poznan riots by brute force; at least fifty-three people were killed and hundreds wounded. Order had been restored, but the regime suffered a staggering blow. Here were workers taking to the barricades against a communist government, with slogans which echoed the nationalist and libertarian sentiments of the hungry nation. The P.Z.P.R. organization was shown to be ineffective, the Army at least partly and the police wholly unreliable. And the P.Z.P.R. itself was now almost openly split from top to bottom between the Stalinists and the progressives.

Yet, when Stalin died in March 1953 Poland appeared to be the most docile and obedient of all the satellites, with no outward signs of opposition. How did the monolithic regime reach a point of disintegration in three short years? The answer, of course, is that the regime was never monolithic and its leaders were only too painfully aware of its weakness and lack of popular support. That was why, when the Russians started dismantling the Stalinist apparatus of terror, the leaders of the P.Z.P.R. were in no hurry to follow suit. It was only well over a year after the execution of Beria that the Polish communists made the first step towards the breaking of the power of their secret police. Other steps followed, grudgingly and slowly, as the pressure for change mounted both within and outside the Party. Gomulka was set free, but the news of his release was not made public for over a year. In January 1955 the P.Z.P.R. officially adopted the policy of 'democratization', but little happened apart from a slight relaxation of censorship and an incomplete purge of the secret police. The regime seemed to be determined to do too little, too late.

Polish intellectuals, faithful to their traditional role of standard bearers in the fight for freedom and independence, were only waiting for a chance to express their non-conformist views. When the chief censor was on holiday in August 1955, the veteran communist poet, Adam Wazyk, fired a broadside from the pages of a literary weekly. In his now famous 'Poem for Adults', he wrote:

Under Socialism
a cut finger does not hurt.
They cut their finger,
they felt pain.
They lost faith.
He ended with a demand
for a clear truth,
for the bread of freedom,
for burning reason,
for burning reason.[1]

The whole editorial board of the weekly was dismissed, but it was too late. Wazyk's poem was circulating throughout the

[1] From a translation by Lucjan Blit in *The Twentieth Century*, London, 1955.

country and other intellectuals were sharpening their pens. Then came the bombshell of Krushev's 'secret' denunciation of Stalin in February 1956, followed immediately by the sudden death of Boleslas Bierut, who on Stalin's orders had replaced Gomulka as First Secretary of the P.Z.P.R. This burst the dam of censorship and Polish intellectuals could indulge in public in an orgy of soul-searching and criticism of the regime.

Edward Ochab, elected in Kruschev's presence to replace Bierut, spoke of hysteria among some party members and made public Gomulka's release. Still afraid of the situation getting out of hand, the P.Z.P.R. continued to move slowly and with extreme caution. An amnesty and a further purge of the secret police in April, the resignation of Jacob Berman in May. . . . This was neither fast enough, nor drastic enough for the people at large, who were suffering from a fall in the already very low living standards, caused by the misguided policies and blunders of the regime.

The Poznan riots exploded at the end of June and led to a slight quickening of the tempo of change. A promise of a 30 per cent increase in wages under a new five-year plan announced in July, a statement that Gomulka had been re-admitted to the P.Z.P.R. and the significant appointment of one of his supporters, General Komar, to command the Internal Security Corps, in August. That month also brought a demonstration of the hold exercised by the Church, when at least a million pilgrims assembled at Czestochowa for the celebrations of the three-hundredth anniversary of the Virgin Mary being proclaimed 'the Queen of Poland'.

September brought a session of the Seym with speeches demanding elected, responsible and controlled leadership, while the press started to discuss quite openly the weaknesses of the communist system and hint that relations between Poland and the Soviet union were perhaps not as equal as they should be. On 9th October, Hilary Minc, the economic dictator of Poland since Stalin's days, resigned from the Government, and a week later it was announced that Gomulka, together with three of his associates, would attend the forthcoming Plenary Session of the Central Committee of the P.Z.P.R. (Plenum for short).

Even before this announcement it must have been plain for all to see that a powerful group within the Party leadership was preparing for Gomulka's return to power. We know now that both the First Secretary, Ochab, and the Prime Minister, Cyrankiewicz, were working in that direction. The Stalinists, thoroughly alarmed by the turn of events, prepared to arrest Gomulka and his supporters, but the news of the plot leaked out and the workers of Warsaw were mobilized in defence of the pro-Gomulka faction. At the same time the Soviet Army in Poland started threatening 'manœuvres'.

That was the situation in Warsaw on the morning of 19th October 1956 when the 8th Plenum assembled and simultaneously Kruschev and his party arrived in the Polish capital. Ochab opened the proceedings by announcing that the Politbureau proposed to co-opt Gomulka and his three associates and then adjourn so that the enlarged Politbureau could meet the Soviet delegation. This was agreed and Gomulka was back in the leadership of the Party before the Russians even had a chance of expressing their views on the matter—the first reassertion of Polish independence.

The meeting between the Polish and Soviet communist leaders was, of course, in private, but enough was said about it during the subsequent proceedings of the resumed P.Z.P.R. Plenum (and an almost complete record of these has been published in Warsaw) and enough leaked to the press by those present, to allow us to reconstruct the main outline of what took place. Judging by all accounts the discussion was a stormy one. The Russians, plainly rattled by the mounting and open tide of anti-Soviet feelings, called the Poles traitors who had sold out to the Americans. In Kruschev's view the Polish 'democratization' was inevitably leading to anarchy, a downfall of communism in Poland and an open breach with the Soviet Union. He was not prepared to watch these developments idly. Public criticism of the Soviet Union had to stop forthwith, the opposition had to be crushed and discipline restored by harsh measures. The Soviet Union would if necessary, ensure this by force. If the Poles wanted to have Gomulka and one or two of his friends in the Politbureau, they could please themselves, but this was no time to change the entire leadership. Trusted and tried men, like Marshal Rokossovsky, had to remain in power.

On the Polish side most of the talking was done by Ochab. He agreed that the situation was serious, but proposed measures diametrically opposed to what Kruschev wanted. Repression would only precipitate revolt. The only way to control the situation was for the Party to put itself at the head of the revolutionary forces and steer them in the right direction, but this could be achieved only if the leadership of the party passed into the hands of men who commanded popular support. The composition of the Politbureau was a purely internal Polish matter and the Russians should not interfere. In future Polish-Soviet relations would have to be based on equality and the Soviet economic exploitation of Poland had to cease.

Kruschev was adamant, and angry exchanges continued for many hours. At one stage, when deadlock was reached, Gomulka threatened to broadcast to the nation and expose the situation in public. Still Kruschev would not budge. Yet in the end he did change his mind. He must have been influenced by reports reaching him through Rokossovsky, that the Polish Army, half a million strong, could not be relied upon to obey Russian orders and might side with Gomulka, who already had the powerful Internal Security Corps on his side. This meant that Kruschev could have his way only at the risk of a major war across his communication lines with Eastern Germany, and this he was not prepared to do.

Suddenly all smiles, the Russians agreed to the Polish plan of action and departed. The P.Z.P.R. Plenum resumed its meeting, listened to a speech by Gomulka and elected a new Politbureau, with Gomulka as First Secretary. All the hard Stalinists, including Rokossovsky, lost their seats. The revolution within the P.Z.P.R. had succeeded. It now remained for the Party to place itself at the head of the popular revolution and steer it clear of the rocks—the rocks of abandoning communism and breaking with the Soviet Union.

Gomulka's speech delivered only a few hours after Kruschev had gone, was dignified and moderate in tone, but it pulled no punches:

'When I addressed the November Plenum . . . seven years ago I thought that it was my last speech to the members of the Central Committee. Seven years have elapsed since that time . . . these years are a closed chapter of history. I am deeply convinced that that period belongs to the irrevocable past. There has been so much evil in those years. The legacy of that period, inherited by the Party, the working class and the nation in many spheres is more than alarming.'

Gomulka proceeded with a devastating analysis of past mistakes. The general economic policy, which had led to waste and inflation, while placing an intolerable burden on the workers, came first under his fire. Next was the policy of forced collectivization, which resulted in a fall in agricultural production. All this led to the Party finding itself without the support of the working class and, to quote his own words again, 'without the confidence of the working class each of us would represent nothing but himself'. And the way to regain that confidence was to tell the truth. 'It is impossible to hide the truth,' said Gomulka. 'If one is hiding it, truth emerges in the form of a dangerous spectre. . . .' But having told the truth and having regained the confidence of the working class, the Party would also regain 'the moral basis of discharging power on their behalf.'

It was not enough, said Gomulka, to remove the men who had made mistakes, the system itself had to be changed and improved, but this could only be done gradually and no quick results could be expected. In industry management methods would have to be reformed, with a realistic system of costing and pricing, with experiments in giving workers a share in the management of enterprises and material incentives to increase productivity. There was also room for private enterprise and the persecution of the artisans would have to stop.

Gomulka's programme for agriculture was even less Marxist. He declared that peasants must be free from pressure to join co-operatives and the co-operatives themselves must have complete independence. He wanted to see new ideas applied to agricultural co-operation and this called for 'creative, progressive thought, of which no party and no man can hold the monopoly. . . . It is a poor idea that socialism can be built only by communists, only by people professing a materialistic social ideology. . . . Diverse forms of the productive community—this is our Polish road to socialism in the countryside.'

Clearly Gomulka was no dogmatist, but he went further still. 'Even a theory of socialism evolved in the best possible way at any given time, in any given conditions, cannot embrace all the details of life, which is richer than theory. What is immutable in socialism can be reduced to the abolition of the exploitation of

Sigismund's Column in Warsaw restored after the war. It commemorates a militant Roman Catholic King (1587–1632) who tried to conquer Russia

The monument at Grunwald in former East Prussia erected in 1960 on the 550th anniversary of the crushing defeat inflicted there on the Teutonic Knights by the combined armies of Poland and Lithuania

man by man. The roads leading to this goal can be and are different. They are determined by various circumstances of time and place. The model of socialism can also vary. It can be such as that created in the Soviet Union, it can be shaped in the manner we observe in Yugoslavia, it can be different still.'

Here was a declaration of faith of a pragmatic communist, which was acceptable to the majority of Poles. Even more welcome was what he had to say about relations with the Soviet Union: 'These relations ought to be based on mutual confidence and equality of rights, on mutual assistance, on mutual friendly criticism, if such becomes necessary, on wise solutions arising out of the spirit of friendship and socialism. . . . Within the framework of such relations each country ought to have complete independence and freedom, and the right of every nation to rule itself in a sovereign manner in its own independent country ought to be fully and mutually respected. This is how it ought to be and, I should say, how it is beginning to be.'

Here Gomulka had to weigh his words carefully. 'The Party . . .' he said, 'should give a determined rebuff to all the whispers and all the voices which strive to weaken our friendship with the Soviet Union. If in the past not everything in the relations between . . . Poland and the Soviet Union was shaping as we thought it should, today this belongs to the irrevocable past. If there are still problems to be settled, this should be done in a friendly and calm manner . . . and if there is anyone who thinks that it is possible to kindle anti-Soviet moods in Poland, then he is deeply mistaken. We shall not allow the vital interests of the Polish State and the cause of building socialism in Poland to be harmed.'

This then was Gomulka's programme for the 'Polish road to socialism'. It held out the promise of a more liberal, pragmatic and humane regime and a less subservient relationship with Russia. In the heady atmosphere of the 'Spring in October' many Poles, and many foreigners as well, tended to read into his programme more than Gomulka meant. They were to be disappointed later, but for the moment Gomulka and the Party placed themselves firmly at the head of the popular movement for reform.

21

PRACTICALLY UNUSED SOVEREIGNTY

Very soon after Gomulka was elected First Secretary of the P.Z.P.R. on 21st October 1956 and became the effective ruler of Poland he discovered that he had mounted a dangerous nationalist tiger. The hatred of Russia, bottled up for so long under Stalinist terror, was threatening to explode. Thoroughly aroused by the events preceding Gomulka's return to power and having tasted freedom once more, the Poles were ready to shed their blood for complete independence, anxious to settle old scores with Russia. This in itself was dangerous but, given time, Gomulka had a chance of controlling the situation. However time was not on his side; the Hungarian rising struck a deep cord of sympathy among Poles and the brutal Soviet intervention there inflamed feelings to a degree which seemed beyond control.

Gomulka and his associates showed cool courage and wisdom in dealing with the situation and achieved what seemed impossible: almost complete independence of Moscow and the simultaneous stemming of the nationalist tide in Poland. How they did it and what exactly did they achieve, shows in sharp relief the problem of Polish-Soviet relations and helps to explain Warsaw's policy since those dramatic days.

In the evening of 24th October, three days after his return to power, Gomulka made his first public speech to the citizens of Warsaw. Ironically the meeting was held in front of the ugly skyscraper Palace of Culture, Stalin's gift to the people of Poland. Tens of thousands assembled to hear their new leader's sober and unemotional speech, calculated to lower the political temperature. Gomulka assured his listeners that relations between Poland and the Soviet Union had become normal and Soviet troops would return to their bases within two days. All internal Polish problems would be solved in accordance with the new policies of the Party and Government. Then came a warning: The presence of Soviet troops in Poland was necessary as long as 'there are Atlantic Pact bases in Western Germany, as long as the new Wehrmacht is being armed there, and chauvinism and revisionism with regard to our frontiers is fomented there'. In view of this it was particularly important to 'rebuff any attempts at anti-Soviet agitation' in Poland. Finally Gomulka appealed for a return to work and an end to demonstrations.

This was plain speaking. Poland could not afford to find herself once more between the German hammer and the Soviet anvil. As long as Germany represented a danger, if only to the newly regained Polish territories, the Poles could not afford to give up Soviet support and that meant the presence of the Red Army on Polish soil. In other words Gomulka was appealing to his listeners not to commit national suicide.

He was given a great ovation, but a part of the crowd shouted 'Rokossovsky go home!' and there was a sinister chant of 'Katyn, Katyn, Katyn. . . .' That night there were anti-Soviet demonstrations and riots in Warsaw and Wroclaw. It was also the day of the first Russian armed intervention in Hungary. If Gomulka was to control the situation he had to demonstrate that his assertion of normal relations with Russia was more than mere words, and he had to demonstrate it quickly.

Already the previous day his close associate, General Marian Spychalski, became Deputy Minister of Defence, but Rokossovsky was still in the ministerial chair. On 26th October General Spychalski issued an appeal to the armed forces. It began with these words:

'In the great days through which our country and Party are now living, the Polish People's Army stands at the side of the people. Soldiers and sailors, N.C.O.s, officers, generals and admirals, the Party, the working class and the entire community thank you for not failing in the trust they placed in you.' The last sentence was a clear reference to the attitude adopted by the armed forces during the tense days before Gomulka's return to power, when the Russians started their menacing 'manœuvres'.

Three days later it was announced that Marshal Rokossovsky had gone on leave. On 31st October several Stalinist senior officers were dismissed from their posts. On 5th November, the day after the Soviet attack on Budapest, thirty-two senior

Soviet officers in the Polish armed forces were politely dismissed and sent packing. Finally, on 13th November, Rokossovsky 'resigned' as Minister of Defence and was replaced by General Spychalski. The symbol of Poland's military subservience to the Soviet Union was finally removed.

Meanwhile the Hungarian tragedy was taking its course. The new leadership of the P.Z.P.R. was obviously in sympathy with Imre Nagy and repeatedly said so in public, never more explicitly than in an appeal to the nation issued on 2nd November:

'Comrades, Citizens! The Polish nation follows with great emotion the course of the Hungarian events. From the bottom of our hearts we have always been on the side of the Hungarian workers and all those who fought together with them for socialist democratization, against the forces which wanted at any cost to maintain in Hungary the old system of government hated by the people.'

The appeal went on to describe the course of events in Hungary and spoke of the tragic consequences of the policy of the former Hungarian leadership which, instead of complying with the will of the nation, had called in Soviet troops. More recently reactionary elements had begun to gain the upper hand, said the appeal, but the defence of the people's power can be achieved 'by the internal forces of the Hungarian people . . . and not by intervention from without'. (The Russians intervened three days later.)

The second part of the P.Z.P.R. appeal dealt with the situation in Poland, stating that the discipline of the nation had enabled it to shape its relations with the Soviet Union on the basis of 'sovereignty, equality of right and friendship'. Soviet troops were stationed in Poland by virtue of an international treaty and represented a guarantee of the western frontier. 'Here and there', continued the appeal, 'voices can be heard demanding the withdrawal of Soviet Army units from Poland. The leadership of the Party stresses with all the necessary emphasis that such demands in the present international situation are contrary to the most vital interests of the nation and the Polish *raison d'état*.

The appeal ended with a call to the nation to keep calm and 'for the sake of the independence of the country' to give rebuff to all anti-Soviet provocations. Put differently, the continuation of the alliance with Russia was a condition of independence not only because it represented a guarantee against any future German claims, but also because the Soviet Union would not tolerate the existence of an anti-Soviet Poland. Consequently great caution was needed if sympathy for the Hungarians was not to lead Poland outside the limits of her independence. The leadership of the Party did not condone the Soviet action in Budapest, but neither did it dare to condemn it in public. The press was allowed to report truthfully, but not to comment. The Polish *raison d'état* imposed restraint.

The Poles felt angry and frustrated at their inability to come to the aid of the Hungarians. 'We used to be the conscience of history, but now our silence has become *raison d'état*,' bitterly wrote Adam Wazyk. But they could do nothing and the great majority realized that it was not the right moment for quixotic gestures. Still, the anti-Soviet feelings continued to fester and more proof was needed that the new phase of relations with Moscow, proclaimed by Gomulka, was becoming reality.

On 14th November, the day after the dismissal of Rokossovsky, Gomulka, accompanied by the Prime Minister, Cyrankiewicz, and the Head of State, Zawadzki, boarded a train for Moscow. The talks with the Soviet leaders, though conducted in a much less tense atmosphere than the dramatic encounter in Warsaw the previous month, were not easy, with a lot of tough bargaining behind the scenes, but they helped to clear the air.

There was a marked and at first puzzling contrast between the public utterances of the effusive and ebullient Kruschev and the reserved polite brevity of Gomulka. During a Kremlin reception Krushchev delivered a long speech about Polish-Soviet friendship based on equality, also about Hungary, Suez and the world at large. Gomulka answered briefly, confining himself to polite remarks about the current negotiations. These performances were repeated when the Poles in turn gave a reception at their embassy. Again Kruschev spoke at length and with emotion about past mistakes and about different roads to socialism, approving Gomulka's election, promising eternal support to Poland, explaining Soviet actions in Hungary and giving his views on other world problems. Once more Gomulka's reply was brief and to the point. He admitted that as he set out for Moscow there had been anxiety in his mind whether the

Russians 'would fully and properly appreciate the changes which have occurred in our country'. This anxiety, he was glad to say, had proved unfounded and the agreement reached between the two delegations confirmed that the Soviet leaders wished relations between socialist countries to be based on the principles of equality and non-interference.

When a joint communiqué was published at the end of the talks, it explained the contrast between the two leaders' speeches by revealing a deep divergence of views on Hungary. On this subject, it said, 'the delegations had exchanged views', while on other matters, such as Suez, China and the United Nations, and disarmament there was 'unity of views'. Clearly Gomulka had asserted his right to an independent assessment of the events in Hungary. This in itself was significant, but of much greater practical importance were the three major concessions obtained by the Poles.

The first did not cost the Russians much, but it had considerable psychological importance. The Soviet Government agreed to facilitate the repatriation of the many thousands of Polish citizens who for various reasons had not been allowed to return to Poland. In the past the fate of the Poles remaining in the U.S.S.R. had been the cause for much resentment.

The second amounted to confirmation of Polish sovereignty. In future both countries 'would consult each other . . . concerning the stay of Soviet military units on Polish territory, their numbers and composition'. The official communiqué added hopefully: 'the temporary stationing of Soviet military units in Poland can in no way infringe the sovereignty of the Polish State and cannot lead to interference in the internal affairs of the Polish People's Republic. . . . Movements of Soviet military units beyond the places where they are stationed require the consent of the Government of the Polish People's Republic.'

Finally the communiqué announced indirectly the end of the Soviet economic exploitation of Poland. In compensation for deliveries of Polish coal, for which she had paid substantially below world prices, the Soviet Union cancelled Polish debts equivalent to about 500 million U.S. dollars. In addition the Soviet Union gave Poland large credits for the purchase of grain, raw materials and manufactured goods.

Thus Gomulka brought back from Moscow quite a considerable bounty. When a cheering crowd surrounded him at the Central Station, he said just a few words, but they were full of meaning: 'The discrepancy between words and deeds, which frequently occurred in Polish-Soviet relations in the past, has now been liquidated.'

The next ten years showed that this was no empty boast. On several occasions the Polish Government and Party have demonstrated that they had minds of their own and were not afraid to disagree with the Soviet Union. On their part the Russian leaders have been consulting the Poles on every major issue. From being the dangerous odd-man-out of the communist movement, Gomulka has become one of its elder statesmen.

If the Poles have not made more use of their independence, not as much for instance as the Rumanians, it is because of their unfortunate geographic position, which forces them to be grudging hosts to the Soviet Army and makes them entirely dependent on Soviet support against what to them is the ever-present German danger. This is the one legacy of Stalin, who drew the western frontier of Poland, which has and is likely to endure.

A favourite political joke in Warsaw towards the end of 1956 has remained as topical as ever. It took the form of an apocryphical advertisement which said: 'Advertiser willing to exchange practically unused sovereignty for a superior geographic position. Apply to Gomulka.'

22

THE CHURCH AND THE STATE

A walk through the streets of Warsaw is in itself an object lesson in Polish history, character and even the present-day political situation. Following the 1944 rising and the systematic demolition ordered by Hitler, only one enormous heap of ruins was left of the once proud city of 1,300,000 inhabitants. The destruction was total. When the Poles regained Warsaw in January 1945 they found themselves in possession of rubble and a few scarred walls pointing to the sky.

Another nation might have decided to build a new capital on the ruins of the old—it would have been easier, quicker and cheaper (and the country was desperately poor). The Poles resolved to rebuild, stone by stone, everything that was ancient and beautiful in pre-war Warsaw. Using old prints, paintings and photographs they set about their task with fanatical enthusiasm and today much of the capital looks as it used to. The whole district of the Old Town, for instance, has been faithfully reconstructed with its renaissance and baroque houses, the Gothic Cathedral of St. John and half a dozen other churches. The same has been done elsewhere with the old palaces of the nobles, the imposing town houses of the wealthy, churches and monasteries rising again, as if in a desperate attempt to salvage the past and restore the continuity of history after the recent cataclysmic upheavals.

Even street names have been mostly preserved; the long north-south artery, Marszalkowska Street, still starts at the Saxon Gardens (which date back to the disastrous reign of Saxon kings in the eighteenth century), passes through Constitution Square and Holy Saviour Square to end in the Union of Lublin Square, commemorating the Polish-Lithuanian Union of 1569. Where street names have been changed, the results are often incongruous: Stalingrad Road leads into Jagiellonian Street and Lvov Street terminates in Workers' Unity Square.

The most prominent, because it is the tallest, among the many ancient monuments which were lovingly raised from the rubble, is the Column of Sigismund III on the edge of the Old Town. On top of this classic column a bronze statue of the King can be seen holding an enormous cross. Of all Polish monarchs Sigismund III was distinguished by his aggressive Roman Catholicism combined with imperialist designs on Russia. That his statue should rise again in Warsaw during the period of Stalinist terror is somehow symbolic of post-war Poland. Not that the Poles have illusions of being a great power any longer, or—except for the lunatic fringe—can even dream of going to war with the Soviet Union, but because the statue of the most Catholic of Polish kings stands in the capital of what is the most Catholic country in the world.

It was Hitler and Stalin between them who helped to give the Church of Rome the unique position it now occupies in Polish life. Before the last war under two-thirds of Polish citizens belonged to the Catholic Church, but Hitler's massacres of the Jews and Stalin's annexation of the eastern provinces (with their large Greek Orthodox and Uniate population) increased the Roman Catholic majority to over 95 per cent of the total population. But that is not all. Hitler's attempt to turn the Poles into a slave race, followed by Stalin's attempt at ruthless Sovietization, restored to the Church its historical identity with the nation, first established during the period of partitions.

Other factors helped to strengthen this identity. On the whole the Catholic clergy had an excellent record of war-time resistance for which many of them paid with their lives, and the Church emerged with enhanced prestige. The communists, by confiscating the vast church estates, brought the clergy still nearer to the common people. Polish peasants have always been among the most devout in Europe and even in towns the hold of the Church has been considerable; now, with the past in ruins, with the old social order destroyed and old ideas discredited, religion was the one unchanging and unchanged beacon for a nation sailing in the turbulent and hostile waters of the Stalinist post-war world.

After 1948 the Stalinists declared war on the Roman Catholic Church. The opposition parties having been eliminated, the Church was the only force over which they had no control, and by definition it was a force hostile to communism. Various attempts were made to break its power by splitting it, by intimidating the clergy and finally by the arrest of several bishops. The Primate, Cardinal Wyszynski, was interned in a monastery and prevented from exercising his functions.

All these repressive measures, far from damaging the Church, only increased the general hatred of the regime, while helping the Episcopate to acquire a halo of martyrdom. Gomulka, when he came back to power in October 1956, saw not only the futility of the war with the Church, but he also realized that he needed its support in the difficult task of controlling an explosive situation. He ordered the release of the Cardinal.

The day after the second and final Soviet military attack on the Hungarian revolutionaries, Cardinal Wyszynski preached his first sermon in more than three years. Thousands filled the vast Church of the Holy Cross in Warsaw, or stood outside listening to his words relayed by loudspeakers. His theme was suffering and love and his thesis: the Poles knew how to die splendidly, but now they had to learn how to work splendidly. 'A man dies once and is quickly covered with glory, but he lives for long years in difficulty, in hardship, pain and suffering, and that is a greater heroism; and just that greater heroism is called for in these times, on this day so pregnant with events and so full of anxiety on all sides.'

The Primate had spoken and the nation obeyed. The oldest and the strongest spiritual power in the land joined Gomulka in his effort to save Poland from a holocaust; together they succeeded. A happy honeymoon between the Church and the State followed, Poland becoming the first communist country to practise complete religious freedom. This co-operation between the Church, demanding total acceptance of its idealistic doctrine, and the State, insisting on the acceptance of Marxist dogma, was unlikely to continue. It could last only if it were possible to draw a clear dividing line between the spiritual realm of the Church and the temporal realm of the State, and no such line can be drawn. Soon the communists and the clergy found themselves in conflict once more. They clashed over religious instruction in schools, over abortion laws, over atheist propaganda and a host of other problems.

The battle about religious instruction in schools illustrates how these conflicts are aggravated by the weakness of the communist regime on the one hand and the unyielding attitude of the Episcopate on the other. By an agreement reached between the Government and the Episcopate in December 1956 religious instruction was reintroduced into schools on a voluntary basis. Ninety-five per cent of all parents requested that their children should be taught religion[1] and almost overnight education in Poland was transformed from an entirely secular into an almost entirely religious one. The pressure of public opinion was such that even children of atheist members of the party had to ask their parents to put them down for religious instruction in order to avoid being ragged, if not victimized, by their class-mates.

The party took fright. At first it tried to fight back by supporting the Society for Secular Schools, but the results were negligible. Administrative pressure followed, while at the same time some prelates went as far as to suggest that if the State was unhappy about religion being taught side by side with Marxism then the setting up of confessional schools would be the ideal solution. In 1960 the Government instructed headmasters to decide in each case if religion was to be taught in their school. The intention was clear and religious instruction was discontinued in nearly 80 per cent of all schools. Parents and children demonstrated in protest, but the Party stuck to its guns. The Church replied by organizing religious instruction on Church premises and, realizing that all control was slipping away, the Party struck the next blow. A new Education Act passed by the Seym in July 1961 proclaimed firmly that schools were secular and must inculcate the 'scientific view of life'—this meant the end of all religious instruction in schools. At the same time the Act placed all forms of education and training outside the schools under the control of the Ministry of Education.

A long and bitter struggle developed over this control. Before leaving for the Vatican Council, Cardinal Wyszynski said in an address to the people of Warsaw (23rd September 1963): 'My dear children. Priests throughout Poland are now being subjected to penalties for teaching catechism without registering and without reporting on their teaching. In a short and very

[1] Hansjakob Stehle: *The Independent Satellite*, London, 1965.

carefully worded letter which was read from the pulpits, we explained that we could not make reports on what a priest teaches the children who are sent to him by their parents. When Christ said, "Go into the whole world and preach the Gospel", he was speaking to priests and bishops, not to government officials. No one may stand between Christ and his bishops and priests; no secular authority has the right to do so. No one may control and inspect them when they do their duty under God . . . we have to obey God rather than man.'[1]

'We have to obey God rather than man . . .' these words are typical of the speaker. Nobody can doubt the integrity of Cardinal Wyszynski. He is totally devoted to the tenets of his religion and would be better cast in the role of a martyr than in that of a prince of the Church, who has to exercise diplomacy. Wyszynski does not mince words and he is a thorn in the flesh of the communist rulers of Poland. In a sermon to clergy from Gdansk during their pilgrimage to Czestochowa in August 1961 he said: 'Compare the two philosophies, these two moral systems, and you will see that you are the most *progressive* people in Poland.'

In a sermon commemorating the 600th anniversary of the Jagiellonian University in Cracow three years later he told his congregation: 'When they tell you that we are already on the pinnacle of achievement, do not believe it! When they tell you that man has already said all that he can say, that we have the best system, a complete ideology, a perfect philosophy, the last word in economics, do not believe it! A student who seeks the truth from his teachers performs a kind of vivisection on them to ascertain whether they are free or merely purveyors of official truths.'

After attending the first session of the Vatican Council he told the clergy in Gdansk (12th April 1964) about his conversations with foreign prelates to whom he had described the 'Vigil of Good Deeds' organized in Poland in support of the Council: 'The Council Fathers asked us, "So you can do things like that?" Yes, we can. "Does it mean that your Communists are Catholics?" They are baptized, anyway. "But don't they

[1] This and the following three quotations are taken from *A Strong Man Armed*, speeches by Cardinal Wyszynski translated and selected by A. T. Jordan, London, 1966.

stop you?" No comment. "How is it possible?" Very simple, our people pray. "So you must be pious to the point of bigotry?" Perhaps we are—but it suits us, we don't mind.

'Our Communist brothers also went to Rome at the time of the Council. There they were asked, "Why do you continue to fight religion in Poland?" They replied, "If the Church had been defeated, we would not oppose it. Since it still holds fast, we have to fight it." No one fights a corpse.'

Cardinal Wyszynski is determined to see that the Roman Catholic Church in Poland does not become a corpse. He knows that it is strong and wants to make it stronger still. But from the communist point of view the influence of the Church is a danger and a challenge to the whole Marxist concept. The Church is the only organization outside their control and it is engaged in the fight for the soul of Poland. In spite of all the administrative harassment of the Church and the honest protestations of the Episcopate, the Roman Catholic Church in Poland has not only more followers, but more churches, parish priests and bishops than ever before, it has the only Catholic university in the communist world, it has its own newspapers and publishing houses, and there are deputies in the Seym who speak on its behalf. The Church is the greatest power in Communist Poland. In this lies both its strength and its weakness.

Strength because the communists know that they cannot destroy the Church and dare not challenge it in a head-on clash (they tried in 1966 in connection with the Millennium celebrations and the Church emerged triumphant). Weakness, because by presenting a danger to communism it faces the rulers of Poland with the unenviable dilemma of either surrendering, or embarking on the long and perhaps hopeless task of working for a slow and gradual erosion of the Church so that future generations might perhaps give their loyalty to Marx and his doctrine.

Cardinal Wyszynski said almost in so many words (in the last sermon quoted) that the communist regime is fighting the Church because the Church is so strong. It is also arguable that the strength of the Church is one of the reasons, if not the main reason, why Gomulka, having inaugurated in 1956 an era of freedom unprecedented in any communist country, soon tightened the reins and allowed other communist countries to overtake Poland in liberalization. For in no other communist country, not even in Hungary, is the Roman Catholic Church either so strong or so identified with national aspirations, to be the natural rallying point for all the forces opposed to communism and in no communist-ruled country is communism itself as weak as it is in Poland.

Does this mean that the Church and the State in Poland are condemned to an endless struggle in which neither dares to challenge the other openly? Perhaps. Both sides, while determined not to surrender their positions, know that overt confrontation can only lead to deadlock or to disaster; they also realize that it is in the interest of each of them to keep the temperature of the conflict as low as possible. And in this lies the hope, if not of an entirely peaceful co-existence, then at least of non-belligerency.

23

THE GREAT LEAP FORWARD

In private the Poles are fond of saying that difficulties are the only permanent feature of their economy. In public they proclaim with pride the great economic achievements of the regime. The average Pole in 1963 (according to official statistics) was 130 per cent better off than his pre-war counterpart, eating two and a half times as much meat and three times as much sugar, buying over twice the quantity of textiles he was able to afford in the bad capitalist days. Have the Poles then achieved an economic miracle in spite of the immense destruction and dislocation caused by the last war?

The answer is not easy to give, for in Poland's case comparisons with pre-war are almost meaningless, if not misleading. After all Poland is today a different country, retaining only just over half of her old territory, 80,000 square miles out of a total of 150,000. The Soviet Union annexed 70,000 square miles of the eastern provinces, mostly poor, with little industry, a largely primitive agriculture and only two big cities, Vilno and Lvov. In compensation Poland was given 39,000 square miles of former German territories, the so called Regained Western Provinces, which included the important Silesian industrial region and the port of Stettin, and also the former Free City of Gdansk. Thus with a stroke of the pen Poland became a smaller (by about a fifth) but theoretically much richer country. Though the regained territories accounted for only between 6 and 7 per cent of all German pre-war industrial production, their inclusion into the predominantly agricultural economy of Poland should have increased the industrial potential of the latter by about half.

On the other hand the regained territories had suffered even greater devastation than old Poland. When the Poles occupied them at the end of the war they found most of industrial enterprises destroyed. And as for agriculture, war operations, fleeing Germans and advancing Russians between them slaughtered or carried away over 90 per cent of the livestock. The land taken over from the eight million Germans, who used to live there prosperously before the war, was a wasteland of desolation.

The task of colonizing these territories, rebuilding the cities, mines, factories, railways and harbours, was perhaps even more daunting than the problem of reconstruction in the rest of the country. And the situation was made desperate by the shortage of trained managers, administrators, scientists, engineers and all kinds of skilled labour. Superimposed on all these difficulties was the rigid system of over-centralized planning and control, copied from Russia, with over-ambitious national plans and an absolute priority for the heavy industry.

It is remarkable that in spite of these formidable handicaps the Poles have managed to achieve as much as they did. Twenty years after they came into possession of the western territories there are again eight million people living there, of whom fewer than a million are the original inhabitants; 1·7 million have come from the eastern provinces annexed by the U.S.S.R., over 2 million from other parts of Poland and nearly 3·5 million were born in the western territories since 1945.[1]

All over Poland frenzied work of reconstruction and construction transformed a basically backward agricultural community into a predominantly industrial society. The turning point came around 1951, when the value of industrial production for the first time exceeded the value of agricultural output.

Share of national income created by industry and agriculture as percentage of total

Year	*1947*	*1951*	*1956*	*1963*
Industry	34	40	43	50
Agriculture	47	37	28	21

The percentage of the population employed in agriculture has also fallen dramatically, from more than two-thirds before the war to well under half by 1960. Simultaneously Poland saw a parallel expansion of the town population at the expense of the countryside.

In many respects Poland did make gigantic strides since the

[1] W. Poznanski: 'The Polish Western Territories', article in *Poland and Germany*, Vol. IX, No. 4, London, 1965.

war. Total industrial production is claimed to be over ten times higher than in 1938, but in spite of all this progress Poland still remains a poor and in many ways a backward country. In the generation of electric power and in the production of crude steel, cement and sulphuric acid per head of population she is running at about half the level achieved by the German Federal Republic. In consumer durables the contrast is, of course, much more striking: during 1965 Poland built only 26,400 motor-cars and, according to latest available figures, there were in the whole country only 211,200 private cars in 1964. But for each motor-car Poland had twelve horses.

An illustration of the low standard of living was provided by an inquiry conducted by the Central Statistical Office early in 1966. According to its findings the main items of expenditure of an average family accounted for the following percentage of income:

	Salary earners	*Wage earners*
Food	48	55
Clothing	15	15
Rent, fuel, electricity	11	9

The small proportion of family income spent on housing can be explained by the very low level of controlled rents and the shocking standard of accommodation. The last census (in 1960) showed that Poles live at the average of 1·7 persons per room, that fewer than one in three dwellings had piped water supply, fewer than one in five had a W.C. and fewer than one in seven had a bath. It will take a long time before Poland even begins to approach the standards of the western countries.

Since Gomulka took over in 1956 there have been efforts to improve the living standards. For two years running, in 1957 and in 1958, the output of consumer goods rose faster than that of capital goods, something unprecedented in post-war Polish development, but since 1959 the priority has been restored to capital goods. However, increased imports from abroad have been helping the consumer. Between 1956 and 1963 the imports of tea, cocoa, citrus fruit and rice trebled in volume, while imports of pharmaceuticals and footwear rose by about 100 per cent, and there have been massive purchases of wheat abroad. At the same time exports of butter, eggs, meat products and sugar shot up, but in spite of this Poland has become a net importer of food, while industrial products form the bulk of her exports.

As in other communist countries, agriculture has been the Achilles' heel of the economy. An official publication puts it tactfully: 'Exceptionally poor crops in 1951–1953 as well as errors in farm policy restricted somewhat the development of agricultural production. . . . But farm policy has undergone essential changes . . . especially since 1956. Measures were introduced aimed at increasing state aid so as to accelerate agricultural production and lighten the farm burdens arising from obligatory deliveries and taxes.'[1]

Socialist pride prevents the authors of this publication from mentioning the most important measure introduced by Gomulka—the end of forced collectivization. Though its slow progress had been one of the distinguishing characteristics of Polish communism, the speed with which collective farms disappeared after 1956 illustrated their unpopularity with the peasants. When Gomulka rose to make his speech to the 8th Plenum of P.Z.P.R. there were about 10,500 collective farms; six months later there were only some 1,700 left and that number dwindled to 1,300 during the next few years.

Apart from those remnants, and some 6,000 State farms established mainly in the Western Territories, the rest of the agriculture is in private hands. There are over 3½ million private holdings, the majority of them small, under 12 acres, and the situation is not altogether unlike the pre-war structure of land tenure. The war, changes in frontiers, and twenty years of communist government have made little impact on the Polish peasant. He may be slightly better educated and he may have somewhat better tools at his disposal, but he remains a suspicious, conservative individualist, who resents innovation and likes to follow the ways of his fathers.

There is no doubt that the peasant is better off today than ever before and the changes introduced under Gomulka have made it worth his while to deliver his produce to the towns. Consequently food supplies in Poland are better, and much less subject to sudden fluctuations, than probably in any other communist country. But the fact remains that agricultural

[1] *Poland in Figures*, Warsaw, 1964.

production is very inefficient and the productivity of the peasants extremely low.

Gomulka is very conscious of this problem. Having abandoned collectivization as a goal for the foreseeable future, he has tried to stimulate the development of Agricultural Circles which own farm machinery on a co-operative basis. Some progress has been achieved and in 1964 there were 30,000 of these Circles with a membership exceeding one million—a large figure yet a disappointing one if one considers that, in spite of considerable financial help given to the Circles by the State, two-thirds of the peasants have refused to join. Worse still, the Circles between them own only 45,000 tractors, which are seldom properly maintained and consequently often out of action. Nor do they possess many of the implements which make a tractor useful. Yet much increased food production is essential if Poland, without spending precious foreign exchange, is to feed her population which grows at the rate of 350,000 per annum. How this will be achieved is one of the unresolved problems facing the regime.

The industrial front presents a more encouraging, though by no means an untroubled picture. After the war the Poles nationalized all large and medium industry and took over the bulk of the distributive system. The whole economy was administered in accordance with a rigid, centrally drawn up five-year plan. The fulfilment of the plan became dogma, irrespective of whether the goods were wanted or not and whether their quality was acceptable. While centralized planning worked, if badly, as far as major industrial projects were concerned, such as the building of vast steelworks or power stations, when applied to lighter industry, especially consumer goods, the system led to bureaucratic waste and chaos of the first order.

By 1956 most Poles had proved to their own satisfaction that communist economy on the Moscow model was inefficient. They also knew from pre-war experience, when the country's wealth barely increased between 1913 and 1938, that classic capitalism did not work in their conditions. What should they do?

In order to improve the lot of the consumer they had to allow a certain expansion of private enterprise—shops, small workshops and what they called 'artisan industry'. Co-operative enterprises were also encouraged. This, together with the abandonment of collective farming, has resulted in Poland having a lower proportion of the population employed in the nationalized sector than any other communist country (in 1965—Poland 26·5 per cent compared with 44·5 per cent in Czechoslovakia and 45 per cent in Eastern Germany). No doctrinaire communist could be happy about this. And could they find an efficient solution for the even more vital problem of the nationalized part of the economy?

They searched for an answer, but when they found it they dared not act on it with speed and resolution. The answer was offered by no less a man than Professor Oscar Lange, member of the Central Committee of the P.Z.P.R., who was made Chairman of a new body, the advisory Economic Council, set up in 1956. Lange, a Reader of economics at Cracow before the war, had spent some years in the U.S.A., first as a refugee and later as communist Poland's first Ambassador in Washington. A lifelong Marxist, he had been on the left wing of the P.P.S. until its merger with the P.P.R.

Lange's prescription for Poland's economic ills, put forward in 1956 and not yet fully implemented, was indeed revolutionary for a communist country. According to him the central planners should not concern themselves with details, but only lay down general targets and main guide-lines of development. It was not up to them to decide how many baking tins or needles were to come on the market, but how the resources of the country should be divided between investment and consumption, and which investments should have priority. Lange also advocated drastic decentralization, with the managers of individual enterprises being given more authority and responsibility, thus removing the need to refer the most trivial decisions to Warsaw. More important still, Lange proposed introducing profitability as the criterion of productivity of individual enterprises, and this meant the introduction of realistic pricing of all goods and commodities.

To orthodox communist ears such views sounded like heresy. (It was only a few years later that the Russian Professor Lieberman startled the Soviet bloc by expressing similar views.) It is not surprising therefore that Gomulka and his colleagues, though they accepted Lange's plan in principle, did not dare to implement it in full. Their policy has been hesitant and they allowed themselves to be overtaken by Czechoslovak and other communists, who embarked on the road of reform much later. However, by 1966 most of Lange's prescription had been put into effect, at least on paper.

So far the statistical success of the communist economy has been fantastic, but statistics do not dwell on quality or on the cost of production. And cost and quality have been the weak points of Polish industry, with expensive machines lying idle for preventable reasons, with long production runs of shoddy or ill-designed goods which nobody wanted to buy, with waste not even a rich country could afford. The latest reforms, which introduce a semblance of realistic costing and profitability accounting in State enterprises, with more freedom for managers and less central planning, promise a much needed improvement. In the final analysis, however, the success of the economy will depend not only on the system, but also on the men who administer it, and a shortage of skilled managers will remain for some time a limiting factor of the Polish industrial leap forward.

24

A HALF-FREE SOCIETY

> Freedom is the highest good of humanity, and free rational activity is the basic condition for the meaning of existence.
>
> Leszek Kolakowski, 1959

> Freedom is a no less important condition of development of man than the satisfaction of his material needs.
>
> Adam Schaff, 1962

The above quotations from the writings of Poland's two leading Marxist philosophers reflect one of the basic popular demands which brought Gomulka back to power. In the heady days of the 'Spring in October' many people believed that the country was entering an era of an unfettered freedom of expression. Having overlooked some of the harsh realities of the situation they were soon to be disappointed. Gomulka was not a western liberal, but a fighting communist, albeit a pragmatic one, who did not return to the leadership of the Party in order to preside over its dissolution. Even if he wanted to, the Russians would not have allowed him to abolish the communist rule, nor would they let him take Poland out of the Warsaw Pact, as Nagy discovered at his cost in Hungary.

However, one of the first measures introduced by Gomulka looked like the beginning of real parliamentary democracy. He had the electoral law changed, and when polling took place in January 1957 the people, for the first time ever in a communist country, had a choice of candidates, a limited choice, but a genuine one. The law stated that in each constituency the number of candidates should exceed the number of seats, though by no more than two-thirds. True, the voters were still presented with single lists of candidates put forward by the communist dominated Front of National Unity, but if they did not like the names of those heading the list, they could cross them out, thus voting on candidates lower down, who represented the other two parties or were described as 'independents'. On the eve of the election Gomulka, having given the limited freedom of choice, took fright at what the electorate might do with it, and in a broadcast to the nation uttered this stern warning: 'To cross out the candidates of our party means to cross out the independence of our country, to cross out Poland from the map of European States.'

The Poles understood the warning: by order of Moscow their government had to be dominated by the P.Z.P.R. They understood, they obeyed, and yet they demonstrated their feelings in a subtle way. The P.Z.P.R. got its majority, but many of its candidates had the lowest number of votes and one even failed to be elected in the first ballot. The resulting Seym had the following composition:

P.Z.P.R. (communist)	237 deputies
Z.S.L. (peasant)	119 deputies
S.D. (democrats)	39 deputies
Non-party	63 deputies, among them 12 Catholic 'leaders'

This pattern has prevailed ever since, with slight fluctuations governed not by the vote of the electorate but by the P.Z.P.R. bosses who dictate the composition of the lists of candidates. The electoral law was changed again in 1960, reducing somewhat but not abolishing the choice offered to the voters, and the composition of the Seym has not changed significantly during the subsequent two elections. The P.Z.P.R. continues to have an absolute majority and all the other deputies, whether members of the remaining two parties or independents, have to acknowledge the leadership of the P.Z.P.R. and support the communist system.

This does not mean, however, that the Seym, like the Supreme Soviet, is just a faceless forum for official speeches and a mere rubber stamp for legislation. The deputies in the Seym do conduct genuine debates, they do examine critically Government bills and introduce amendments, occasionally they abstain, or even vote against the Government. The Catholic deputies of the *Znak* are particularly outspoken and show the greatest independence. In theory the Seym can overthrow the Government, in practice it is a debating forum with an influence on marginal issues only, not allowed to question major lines of policy or the system itself.

By contrast the private individual enjoys much greater freedom. He can say what he likes in private without fear of arrest or persecution, he can grumble about the iniquities of bureaucracy in public. He is free to join the Party or stay outside (the P.Z.P.R. has only just over 1½ million members) but if he is an ambitious opportunist or—that rare animal—a genuine Marxist, he will of course join. He can without permission change his job and his place of residence, though the desperate shortage of accommodation makes the latter difficult in practice. If he has the money he can even join a housing association and, with Government help, have his own small house built.

It is not very difficult for him to start a small business as long as he does not employ many other people, but should he be a lawyer, he will not longer be allowed to indulge in private practice but will have to become a member of a co-operative. If he is an employee, he will find it very difficult to make ends meet on his wages or salary; his wife will have to go out to work, or he will have to take a second spare-time job, unless he can indulge in profitable pilfering in his factory.

Should he want to travel abroad, he has to run the gauntlet of police bureaucracy to obtain a passport. The outcome is uncertain, but the odds are in favour of his getting one. If the West is his destination he will have to be invited by kind friends or relatives who will also have to pay for his ticket; he himself will be allowed to take out of the country only five U.S. dollars, unless he is travelling on official business. In spite of these difficulties more than 50,000 Poles manage to visit the West every year, while travel within the communist bloc is relatively easy.

A Pole who is unable to go abroad need not be cut off from the outside world. He can listen to foreign stations, including the Polish services of the B.B.C. and the Voice of America (jamming was abolished in 1956) without fear of persecution. If he is lucky and persistent he might get hold of one of few copies of foreign newspapers which are on sale in Warsaw and some other big cities. On the other hand he should have no difficulty in seeing foreign films—about a hundred of them are bought each year from the West and a similar number from communist countries. During his visits to the cinema—on the average he goes six times a year—he can demonstrate his political predilections as well as his taste in entertainment, by favouring films of one origin or another. An analysis of cinema attendances in 1960 makes illuminating reading.[1]

Country of origin	*No. of films (old and new)*	*Performances in thousands*	*Audiences in millions*	*Average no. of people who saw each film in thousands*
E. Germany	54	37	4·0	65
U.S.S.R.	245	305	30·0	125
Italy	69	86	9·9	140
W. Germany	38	48	5·5	145
France	172	241	32·9	190
Britain	55	122	15·0	270
U.S.A.	58	144	32·9	560

The Pole, if he is a theatregoer (there are 130 theatres and concert halls in the country) has the choice of native and foreign plays ranging from the classics to Duerrenmatt, Beckett, Arthur Miller and Edward Albee. If he reads books (more than 8,000 titles published in 1964) he has a fair choice of translations—178 from English, 166 from Russian, 68 from German, 50 from French and 21 from the Scandinavian languages).[2]

The educated Pole can be, and on the whole is, remarkably well informed about the outside world and the main currents of thought in the West. Ultimately however, what he reads or sees on the stage or in the cinema is controlled by the Party. Censorship of all forms of public expression has continued and, like all Polish internal policy, it has followed a zigzag course. The first crack of the whip came soon after the euphoria of 1956, with the suppression in 1957 of the most outspoken weekly, *Po Prostu*, which had played a significant part in bringing Gomulka back to power.

Gomulka himself is anything but an intellectual and views

[1] Table based on official statistics quoted in H. Stehle, *The Independent Satellite*, London, 1965.

[2] U.N. Statistical Yearbook, 1965.

philosophers and writers of all sorts with considerable suspicion. He knows that they have a long tradition of outspoken rebellion and he has found controlling them as difficult as riding a wild horse. In many ways the situation resembles the conflict between the Church and the State, though the intellectuals cannot command anything like the mass support enjoyed by the Episcopate. Gomulka's concern is to strengthen communism in Poland (he knows it to be only wafer thin at present) and he tries to draw a line beyond which freedom of expression must not go. The intellectuals regard freedom as indivisible. Result: a protracted confrontation between the Party and the intellectuals; the Party restrictive but reluctant to embark on a policy of harsh suppression, the intellectuals smarting under the restrictions and vocal in their protests.

In March 1964, after the Party had closed down two lively cultural weeklies, *Przeglad Kulturalny* and *Nowa Kultura*, replacing them by the dull and timid *Kultura*, thirty-four leading intellectuals sent a letter to the Prime Minister, Joseph Cyrankiewicz. They objected to the tightening up of censorship and the discriminatory allocation of paper for books and periodicals, a less obvious but equally effective method of controlling the circulation of publications regarded as objectionable. The letter, though it was never published in Poland, caused a considerable stir, without bringing any desirable results. Discreet punishment fell on the signatories, who were deprived of their passports and for a time prevented from publishing their books or contributing to the press and radio. When public opinion abroad took up the cry, two of the writers who had signed the letter were arrested and sentenced to terms of imprisonment for transmitting abroad matter 'slanderous to Poland', but the sentences were suspended.

Intellectuals who are also Party members can be a source of profound embarrassment for the leadership. In October 1966, at a meeting held in Warsaw to evaluate the achievements of the past decade, Professor Leszek Kolakowski delivered a speech in which he drew unfavourable comparisons between the intellectuals' hopes in 1956 and the reality ten years later. The Party reacted by expelling Professor Kolakowski, but he was allowed to continue teaching at the university.

This is symbolic of the attitude of the Party to all intellectuals.

Slawomir Mrozek, the most original playwright and satirist of the younger generation has been allowed to live in Italy, while his works, which have questioned practically every dogma under the sun, continue to be performed and published in Poland, though not immune from the censor's interference. A powerful novel about the Spanish Inquisition (which could be taken as a comment on Stalinism) by Jerzy Andrzejewski, the author of *Ashes and Diamonds*, was a great success with the public, but not allowed to appear in a second edition and a play based on it was taken off after a short provincial run. (Incidentally, both Mrozek's and Andrzejewski's works have won acclaim in the West and have been translated into English, German and other languages.) From a writer's point of view the uncertain and erratic behaviour of the authorities can sometimes be even more frustrating than a stricter, but predictable censorship.

Only in music, painting, sculpture and architecture does the Party impose no restrictions. Having turned its back on 'socialist realism' it does not officially frown on any style or absence of style. Composers and painters have not been assigned any social tasks, they are not really expected to contribute to the socialist education of the nation. Since their works cannot undermine the communist system, they are allowed full freedom and make an excellent use of it. Their unfortunate fellow-intellectuals, who deal in words and ideas, can only look on them with envy.

Is this half-freedom a permanent feature of the Polish system? By its very nature half-freedom is a most unstable condition and satisfies nobody, but whether it will move towards fuller freedom or stricter control, depends on very many factors. A part of the P.Z.P.R. leadership, and the overwhelming majority of the intellectuals hope that in the long run freedom of expression will prevail, but this assumes a similar development in the Soviet Union. It also implies a convergence between the eastern and the western systems and an evolution of communism towards a new kind of society, which, though not a copy of western models, yet resembles them in many respects.

There is hope that the next generation of the country's leaders, the students and university graduates of the post-war period, for whom the harsh conflicts of the thirties and forties are not even a memory, will have a healthily pragmatic approach to Poland's problems. Opinion polls conducted among students between

1958 and 1963 have consistently shown that about two-thirds of them favoured some kind of socialism, but only a minority regarded themselves as Marxists. Many of these young people are already on their way to the top.

More recently there have been signs of growing political indifference and apathy among the 200,000 Polish university students. The frustrations of disappointed hopes and of bureaucratic reality, the low standard of living and the restricted intellectual freedom, combined with the knowledge that the Poles themselves can do little about it, are having an affect on the young. An inquiry conducted in 1966 among 734 first-year students of the Cracow Academy of Mines and Metallurgy (and published in the weekly *Zycie Literackie*) threw an interesting, though oblique light on this problem. The inquiry discovered that the students were better informed about the political parties in Britain and the U.S.A. than about the rulers of their country, and a significant number did not even know the position occupied by Gomulka. When asked to name their 'hero' the students gave the largest number of votes to the late President Kennedy; next in popularity came Yuri Gagarin, President de Gaulle, Pope John XXIII and Karl Marx. This poll may reveal certain apathy and ignorance about the present-day realities in Poland, but it shows no lack of political awareness and does seem to point towards convergence with the West.

At the same time the leading Marxist philosophers in Poland are re-examining critically the whole structure of communist ideology, rejecting most of the dogma, quoting in the process George Orwell, and reaching some surprising conclusions. Not only Kolakowski, who has been expelled from the Party, but Professor Adam Schaff, who at the time of writing was still a member of the Central Committee, have been planting high explosive charges under the edifice of orthodox Marxism-Leninism. Professor Schaff in his book *Marxism and the Individual* (published in Warsaw in 1965) has gone a long way towards reconciling Marxism with existentialism, towards a revaluation of the role of the individual and has even admitted that a socialist state is an 'alienating force'.

There can be little doubt that if left alone the Poles would develop a form of socialism which would make not only Stalin but also Lenin turn in their graves. But will they be allowed to do so? Gomulka and his colleagues are casting anxious glances at what is happening in Moscow; they are also haunted by the fear of the anarchic streak in the Polish character. As long as the present men are in power, further liberalization, if any, is bound to be slow and halting.

25

POLAND, THE WORLD AND THE FUTURE

During his official visit to London in February 1967 the Polish Foreign Minister, Adam Rapacki gave a press conference. When the inevitable questions about the Oder-Neisse line was asked, he replied: 'Poland's western frontier is an irrevocable and final fact. We are aware of that and do not need any reassurance on this matter.' The Minister was speaking the truth, but not the whole truth. Poland may not be seeking *assurances* in the matter of her western frontier, but what she desperately wants is a genuine, final and formal *recognition* of that frontier by the German Federal Republic and her N.A.T.O. allies. This has been the main preoccupation of Polish foreign policy and is bound to remain so in the future.

However unpopular some of its other policies may be, the Polish Government can rely on overwhelming support when it describes the Oder-Neisse line as 'final', 'immutable' and 'irreversible', and it never misses an opportunity for doing so. The Poles have no feeling of guilt towards the seven or eight million Germans who lost their homes in what are now the Polish western territories—it would be surprising if they did after their experiencse during more than five years of Nazi occupation. But while there is no guilt feeling, the fear of Germany, which is part of the atavistic heritage of every Pole, is very real indeed. The Poles realize also that should a reunited Germany ever lay claim to the lands east of the Oder-Neisse line, they would not be strong enough to defend them alone.

By pushing Poland to the west at the Potsdam conference in 1945, Stalin ensured that the Poles should become prisoners of the Soviet Union, condemned to rely on Russian support against future German territorial claims. The Western Allies, by their (legalistically most proper) insistence that the frontiers drawn up at Potsdam are subject to ratification by the Peace Conference (which has never met), have put bars in the windows of that prison. Successive governments of the German Federal Republic, by their refusal to recognize the Oder-Neisse Line, have added a high wall, which makes escape almost impossible. But the Poles, apart from German territorial claims, have another recurrent nightmare: can they really rely on Soviet support? Memories of the Molotov-Ribbentrop pact and of the partition period do not inspire much confidence on that score.

Even if most Polish leaders understand that responsible Bonn politicians have no desire to embark on any re-conquests, they dare not ignore the danger of revival of German nationalism and imperialism. For a while such fears might have seemed exaggerated, but the recent rise of neo-Nazism in the Federal Republic has tended to confirm the worst Polish suspicions. On 25th February 1967 Prime Minister Joseph Cyrankiewicz addressed a P.Z.P.R. meeting at Wroclaw (Breslau) in the following words:

'During the terms of office of all her three Chancellors, the entire policy of the German Federal Republic has endeavoured to avert the consequences of Germany's military defeat, to abolish the existing territorial system, to revise the existing frontiers, to restore to Germany the status of a big power, to re-open to her the way to a new hegemony of Europe. This is a policy directed against the security and peace of the whole of Europe, though on the face of it it seems to be directed above all against Poland and her frontiers on the rivers Oder and Neisse.'

Cyrankiewicz may have been less than fair to Chancellors Adenauer, Ehrhard and Kiesinger, but he was thoroughly alarmed not only by the rise of the new German nationalist party, the N.P.D. ('The German Federal Republic,' he said, 'has now become the scene of unbridled jingoism, neo-Nazism and revisionism.'), but also by the success of Bonn in establishing normal relations with Rumania and thus breaching the hitherto united communist front against the F.D.R. The rise of nationalism in particular worries the Poles, who have consistently objected to the rearming of Germany, while the mere thought of Bonn acquiring any share in nuclear weapons sends them straight into the arms of the Russians (who share the same anxieties).

It is the fear of Germany which has prevented the Poles from making much use of the nominal independence from Russia that they won in 1956. They have made not the slightest attempt to exploit the Sino-Soviet quarrel and the general disarray in the communist world, but this does not mean that the foreign policy conducted from Warsaw is not formulated primarily in the interest of Poland. It only means that the Poles have singularly little room for manœuvre, less in fact than any other communist government, with the exception of the East German regime.

The Poles look with some envy at the Rumanians' freedom of action and at President de Gaulle's assertion of complete French independence from Washington. (They are, incidentally, grateful to de Gaulle for being the only leading western statesman to come out without any reservation in favour of the Oder-Neisse line). They would very much like to follow a more independent line from Moscow, but they cannot, for their essential interests for the time being coincide completely with those of the Soviet Union.

What then are the aims of Poland's foreign policy. In the short term they can be summed up as follows:

1. The new western frontier must be preserved at all costs. This means that the Federal German Government must be made to recognize it without reservations—the East German D.D.R. did so in 1950.

2. The formal recognition of the Oder-Neisse line will not be worth the paper on which it is written if Germany becomes once more a great military power ruled by nationalists. Consequently Germany must be kept as weak as possible and that means that it must be kept divided. Communist East Germany serves that purpose, provides a useful buffer between Poland and the Federal Republic, and since it could not survive on its own, it has to rely on the presence of Soviet troops on its territory. This gives Poland additional protection against the danger of German revisionism, but it also means the unwelcome presence of Soviet troops in Poland, which sits astride the Russian lines of communication. Though the Russian soldiers in Poland are few and inconspicuous, their presence is a depressing irritant and a blow to national pride. For the time being this is a reasonable price to pay for national security.

3. Since a Soviet-German deal cannot be ruled out in the future it is essential to do everything possible to convince the Russians that their interests are identical with those of Poland. This can only be achieved if Warsaw pursues a genuinely pro-Russian policy and helps Moscow in preserving the unity of the communist countries bordering the Soviet Union in Europe.

In the long term, Poland's only hope of lasting security from Germany and independence from Russia lies in an international *détente*, disarmament, and a generally peaceful world. Hence the Rapacki Plan and all the moves connected with it.

The Rapacki Plan, the only major Polish initiative in the field of international relations since 1945, deserves closer study. Contrary to what some western commentators have said, there can be little doubt that the Plan originated in the Polish Foreign Office. The Russians gave it their blessing only after a great deal of persuasion by the Poles. The Plan, launched formally by Rapacki himself in a speech to the United Nations Assembly in October 1957, called for the establishment of a nuclear free zone, comprising Poland, Czechoslovakia and both the Federal German Republic and the D.D.R.

The idea was received with some interest in the Western circles and four months later Rapacki produced a detailed memorandum on the subject. In the proposed nuclear free zone the governments of the four countries concerned would undertake not to manufacture or acquire nuclear weapons. The great powers, the U.S.S.R., U.S.A., Britain and France, would undertake not to place their nuclear weapons in the territories in question and would renounce the use of nuclear weapons against targets in the zone. There would be a system of international inspection, both on the ground and from the air, with control posts in the zone to ensure the implementation of the undertakings.

For a variety of reasons, not all of them valid, the Western Powers, while showing polite interest and discussing the Plan, did not accept it. Undeterred, the Poles pressed on. In March 1962 Rapacki presented to the Geneva Disarmament Conference a new version, which went further than the original plan. 'The purpose of the Polish proposal,' stated an official memorandum, 'is the elimination of nuclear weapons and nuclear delivery vehicles, a reduction of military forces and conventional armaments in a limited territory, in which this can contribute towards the lessening of tension and a substantial reduction in the danger of conflict in that territory.'

As in the original version, the new plan also applied to Poland, Czechoslovakia and the whole of Germany, but allowed for other countries joining the disarmament zone. Again, the Poles wanted the implementation of this plan to be subject to international control. Like most disarmament proposals, the new Rapacki Plan raised a host of extremely difficult technical questions and was eventually buried under an avalanche of speeches and memoranda.

Having made no progress with this idea, the Poles put forward yet another plan, the Gomulka Plan. In a memorandum, delivered on 29th February 1964, the Polish Government proposed 'the freezing of nuclear and thermonuclear armaments' in the four countries included in the Rapacki Plan. But the Gomulka Plan was even more difficult to implement than the earlier proposals. Again no progress was made. Yet the Polish interest in the lowering of temperature in central Europe and the removal of any threat from Germany remains the imperative of their foreign policy.

Every year at the United Nations Assembly, at the Geneva disarmament talks and at any other suitable opportunity, Polish representatives return to the theme of the Rapacki Plan. It is today, they stress, as valid as ever and the need for it becomes more pressing with each year that passes. The Poles are today probably the most convinced disarmers in Europe, for they realize that their own survival can be assured only in a peaceful world.

They also know that the degree of freedom they will be allowed to enjoy at home will depend even more on the international situation than on the men in charge in Warsaw. Still, the question as to who will succeed Gomulka exercises their minds to an increasing degree. Gomulka is only in his early sixties (he was born in 1905), but his health is poor, his popularity, which used to be enormous, is gone, though his authority remains unchallenged in public. Many of his communist colleagues feel that he should retire. They, and the people at large, are tired of Gomulka's long, boring speeches, of his extreme caution and his lack of vision. Gomulka himself, probably afraid of the anarchic streak which is never far below the surface in Poland, stubbornly continues to follow the orthodox course, but as the twelfth anniversary of his advent to power approaches, the country seems to be ripe for another change of leadership.

Gomulka has no heir apparent and the contenders for his office are many. Edward Gierek, the intelligent and efficient chief of the P.Z.P.R. in Wroclaw, would be the popular choice of many Party members; he is already both in the Politbureau and in the P.Z.P.R. Secretariat, still in his early fifties, clearly a man to be reckoned with. But it is quite possible that Gomulka's retirement, when it comes, will be followed by a period of collective leadership until one man emerges on top. In the wings, however, a somewhat sinister figure is waiting—General Mieczyslaw Moczar, the Minister of the Interior and the leader of the *Zbowid* organisation (Association of Fighters for Freedom and Democracy), which embraces not only ex-combatants and communist partisans, but also former members of the A.K. General Moczar is credited with political ambition and his views are a tough amalgam of nationalism and communism; because of his nationalism he enjoys considerable popularity.

Perhaps afraid of Moczar's growing influence, Gomulka removed the armed Internal Security Corps from the control of the Ministry of the Interior and placed it under the Minister of Defence, Marshal Spychalski. In theory Spychalski, with a seat on the Politbureau and all the armed forces under his orders, could easily grasp the reins of power and set up a semi-military dictatorship, but this is probably the least likely of all the possible solutions.

Whoever inherits Gomulka's mantle will also inherit all his problems. There may be slight changes of emphasis, tactical shifts and adjustments of methods, but major changes of internal or foreign policy can be ruled out as long as the present international situation continues. To quote Gomulka addressing a special session of the Seym, called to commemorate the millennium of Poland: 'The destinies of the Polish nation, its sovereignty and independent existence have been linked for ever with the destinies of socialism.' Many Poles may wince at Gomulka's 'for ever', but no responsible politician can see any alternative, at least in the foreseeable future. However much they may feel that spiritually they belong to the West, however much they may dislike communism and the Russians, they know that they cannot survive if they find themselves once more between the German hammer and the Soviet anvil.

POSTSCRIPT – AUTUMN IN MARCH?

Since this book was written events outside Poland helped to bring into the open grievances and frustrations which have been bottled up under Gomulka's pro-Soviet, conservative-communist regime. The lightning Israeli victory over Egypt in June 1967 was greeted with popular rejoicing because in Polish eyes it meant a defeat for Russia; at the same time many of the few remaining Jews in Poland (the total is estimated at 30,000) rejoiced for more obvious reasons.

Acting in tune with Moscow, Gomulka and his Party administered severe rebukes to the Jews, to the Zionists and to all Israeli sympathizers. 'Zionism' became a term of abuse with anti-semitic overtones. The pro-Israeli attitude was described by the Party as 'a pro-imperialist stand, masked by nationalism'. Even the senior echelons of the armed forces found this line difficult to swallow and the Party ordered a purge which included the Chief of the Air Force.

The next stage came early in 1968 when a further tightening of Polish censorship coincided with the dramatic liberalization in Czechoslovakia. The authorities lit the fuse by banning further public performance of *Dziady*, a play by the great poet Adam Mickiewicz, written under the immediate impact of the brutal suppression of the November rising against the Tsar in 1831. This play, which is not among the poet's masterpieces, contains some strong anti-Russian passages and the Warsaw public applauded them with rapture, while students marched to the monument of the bard. Soon the Warsaw branch of the Writers' Union met in extraordinary session and passed a resolution calling for the restoration of tolerance and freedom of artistic expression and the lifting of the ban on *Dziady*. The writers also voiced their solidarity with their Czechoslovak colleagues.

In March the students in Warsaw and several other major cities demonstrated in the streets with slogans like 'We want freedom!', 'Long live the writers!', 'Gestapo go home!' and

'Long live Czechoslovakia!' The authorities answered with truncheons, tear gas and arrests, but the demonstrations continued. In a desperate attempt to alienate the students from the masses, the Party revived the Zionist bogy and blamed it all on an absurd conspiracy between revisionists, nationalists, Zionists and German imperialists, thus trying to play at the same time on the fear of Germany and on the latent anti-semitism of a large part of the population. Several high officials of Jewish origin were dismissed.

On 20th March Gomulka in a public speech, which was repeatedly interrupted by shouting and cheers in the wrong places, turned his wrath against the intellectuals, singling out several prominent writers of all persuasions. He dwelled at length on the theme of Zionism, but declared that the majority of Jews were loyal citizens. A few days later seven prominent university professors, four of them of Jewish origin, were dismissed for allegedly inciting the students. Among those who lost their chairs was the leading Marxist philosopher, Leszek Kolakowski. Gomulka had clearly decided to stamp out the revolt of the intellectuals, as others have tried before him. But the events in Czechoslovakia have weakened his position and his days seem to be numbered. Unfortunately none of his probable successors offers much hope of liberalization. If there is a Polish Dubcek he has not yet revealed himself, and it seemed that this March Autumn suddenly returned to Poland.

London
March 1968

SELECT BIBLIOGRAPHY

Barnett, Clifford R.: *Poland, Its People, Its Society, Its Culture*, Grove Press, New York, 1958.

Bor-Komorowski T.: *The Secret Army*, Gollancz, London, 1950.

Cambridge History of Poland edited by W. F. Reddaway and others, 2 vols., Cambridge University Press, 1941 and 1950.

Central Statistical Office of the P.P.R.: *Poland in Figures*, Warsaw, 1964.

Dziewanowski, M. K.: *The Communist Party in Poland*, Harvard University Press, Cambridge, Mass., 1959.

Gora, W. and Golebiowski, J. (editors): *Z Najnowszych Dziejow Polski*, P.Z.W.S., Warsaw, 1963.

Hiscocks, Richard: *Poland—Bridge for the Abyss?*, Oxford University Press, London, 1963.

Halecki, Oscar: *A History of Poland*, Dent, London, 1961.

Hartley, J. H. and Wrzos, K.: *Colonel Beck*, Hutchinson, London, 1939.

Kleiner, J.: *Zarys Dziejow Literatury Polskiej*, Ossolineum, Warsaw, 1964.

Machray, Robert: *The Poland of Pilsudski*, Allen and Unwin, London, 1936.

Mikolajczyk, S.: *The Pattern of Soviet Domination*, Sampson Low, London, 1948.

Milosz, Czeslaw: *The Captive Mind*, transl. by J. Zielonko, Secker and Warburg, London, 1953.

Pilsudski, Joseph: *Pisma Zbiorowe*, Warsaw, 1937–39.

Polish Academy of Sciences: *Historia Polski*, 6 vols., P.W.N., Warsaw, 1957–59.

Polish Ministry of Information: *The German New Order in Poland*, Hutchinson, London, [1942?].

Rose, W. J.: *Poland*, Penguin, London, 1939.

Poland Old and New, Bell and Sons, London, 1949.

Schmitt, B. E. (editor): *Poland*, University of California Press, Berkley, 1945.

Stehle, Hansjakob: *The Independent Satellite*, transl. by D. J. S. Thomson, Pall Mall, London, 1965.

Syrop, Konrad: *Spring in October*, Weidenfeld and Nicolson, London, 1957.

Wyszynski, Stefan: *A Strong Man Armed*, speeches translated and selected by A. T. Jordan, Geoffrey Chapman, London, 1966.

Zweig, Ferdynand: *Poland between two Wars*, Secker and Warburg, London, 1944.

INDEX

K

L

M

N

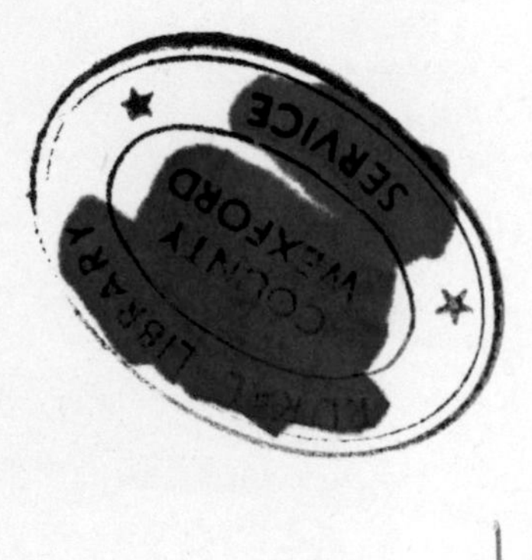
WEXFORD
COUNTY
LIBRARY
SERVICE

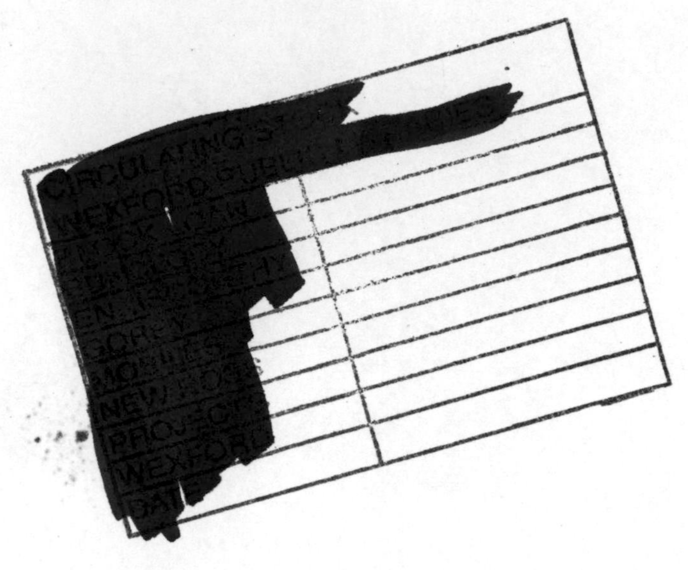